FROM DEATH TO LIFE

From DEATH to *Life*
The Aaron Williams Story

CHRIS WILLIAMS

RISE UP LAZARUS PRINTING | MT. STERLING, KY

From Death to Life: The Aaron Williams Story
By Chris Williams
Published by Rise Up Lazarus Printing, Mt. Sterling, KY

Copyright © 2024 Chris Williams
All rights reserved.

This publication is protected under the U.S. Copyright Act of 1976 and all other applicable international, federal, state, and local laws. All rights are reserved, including resale rights. You are not allowed to reproduce, transmit, or sell this book in part or in full without the written permission of the publisher.

Limit of Liability: Although the author and publisher have made reasonable efforts to ensure that the contents of this book were correct at press time, the author and publisher do not make, and hereby disclaim, any representations and warranties regarding the content of the book, whether express or implied, including implied warranties of merchantability or fitness for a particular purpose. You use the contents in this book at your own risk. Author and publisher hereby disclaim any liability to any other party for any loss, damage, or cost arising from or related to the accuracy or completeness of the contents of the book, including any errors or omissions in this book, regardless of the cause. Neither the author nor the publisher shall be held liable or responsible to any person or entity with respect to any loss or incidental, indirect, or consequential damages caused or alleged to have been caused, directly or indirectly, by the contents contained herein. This book's contents are informational and not legal or tax advice, and the authors and publishers are not engaged in the provision of legal, tax, or any other advice. You should seek your own advice from professional advisors, including lawyers and accountants, regarding the legal, tax, and financial implications of any real estate transaction you contemplate.

For permission requests, write to the publisher, addressed "Attention: Chris Williams, Grass Cuts dba Rise Up Lazarus Printing, 109 Bentbrook Drive, Mt. Sterling, KY 40353"

FRONT COVER DESIGN: Wendy Dunning
INTERIOR DESIGN: Wendy Dunning
PUBLISHING CONSULTANTS: Peter Wietmarschen / Colleen Wietmarschen, https://yourliteraryprose.com / https://theauthorsvoice.org
EDITORS: Peter Wietmarschen / Colleen Wietmarschen

ISBN: 979-8-9903460-0-0 (Hardcover)
ISBN: 979-8-9903460-1-7 (eBook)

Publisher's Cataloging-in-Publication Data
Library of Congress Control Number: 2024905872
Published in the United States of America

Printed in the United States of America

Dedication

*To my grandparents, James Arthur Copher
and Anzy Newsome Copher, hardworking farmers
from whom I learned many life lessons.*

Preface

I had no plans to write this book. People kept telling me to write it because it would benefit others. I started to realize Aaron's story was essential to share, but I doubted my ability to communicate the fears, sorrow, hopes appropriately, and eventual joy experienced. Would I be able to relive what happened? Would I find the strength to adequately share the fear we felt, starting with the phone call informing us of the accident through recovery and the present-day struggles? The new normal for Aaron.

Terrible things happen to everyone, but something good can come from tragedy. The final words were written through the support of my wife, daughter, the community, and, yes, God's guidance.

Foreword

On September 19, 2015, Chris Williams received a call no parent wants to receive. His son, Aaron, had been in a bad accident, and his life was hanging in the balance. While Chris, a minister of the Gospel, a pastor, and a preacher of the Word of God, was a man of faith, his faith was about to be tested at a level he had never experienced before.

As Chris and Veronica arrived at the hospital emergency room, the medical staff told them that very few people survived the type of head injury Aaron had sustained in the wreck. They did not expect him to live through the night, and if he did live, he would most likely be a vegetable for the rest of his life.

While the prognosis was not good, Chris did not despair because he had hope and faith in the Great Physician, almighty God. As a pastor and preacher of many years, he had proclaimed the message of faith in God. He even prayed on behalf of others, believing God for his miraculous touch on them. Chris faced cancer himself and put his faith in God, and God had brought him through. However, this would be a challenge to Chris's faith at a level he had never experienced in the past.

That night, Chris prayed and put his faith in God for Aaron. The call went far and wide, asking people to intercede and pray for Aaron. Soon, heaven was bombarded by people's prayers interceding and asking God for his intervention and healing of Aaron.

I served as the state minister for the Church of God in Kentucky during this time. So, I was Chris's pastor and his friend. I was by his side and stayed in constant contact with him. Every time we connected, I never heard despair or hopelessness in his voice; I never heard a tone that would indicate he was wavering in his faith. Chris believed that God was going to bring Aaron through.

Day after day, Chris prayed and put his faith in God for Aaron. Day after day, the doctors and the family could see God at work in Aaron, healing and restoring him as Aaron had to learn to talk, walk, eat, and do everything a person does daily. People came from far and wide to pray for Aaron. Chris welcomed anyone who came to pray and intercede for his son. People from as far away as Japan flooded Chris's inbox with daily emails for Aaron.

Chris's faith in God for Aaron has genuinely inspired many people. As a result, Chris felt led to write this book to share the story of what faith in God can do, even in the direst circumstances. I am confident that your faith in God will be inspired and strengthened as you read it.

As a minister of the Gospel, people often ask me why we don't see miracles today like those we read about in the Scriptures and Church history. I can tell you that God is still working miracles today because Aaron Williams is, without question, a walking miracle of God.

Chris was a man of faith before Aaron's accident. He lived a life of faith every day. However, after walking through this journey with his son and watching God heal and restore his son when the doctors gave them very little hope, Chris's faith is now far more profound than it has ever been. As you read this book, I am confident your faith will be strengthened.

—Rev. Dr. Darryl Allen, Senior Pastor,
Meade Station Church of God, Ashland, KY
Former State Minister for Kentucky Church of God

Contents

PREFACE
7

FOREWORD
8

Chapter 1
From Accepting Jesus...
12

Chapter 2
...To Bonds of Marriage
16

Chapter 3
From the Love of Sport...
20

Chapter 4
...To a Life-Altering Accident
24

Chapter 5
The First Night From Life-Saving Care...
34

Chapter 6
...To Prayers Around the World
39

Chapter 7
From Relearning Life's Basic Skills...
56

Chapter 8
...To Aaron's Continued Recovery
71

Chapter 9
From Death to Life:
The Aaron Williams Story
76

ACKNOWLEDGMENTS

91

APPENDIX

92

ABOUT THE AUTHOR

103

Chapter 1
From Accepting Jesus...

> "Trust in the Lord with all thine heart; and lean not unto thine own understanding. In all thy ways acknowledge HIM, and HE shall direct thy paths."
>
> PROVERBS 3:5-6

Veronica asked me to attend church one Sunday, and I said, "No." She kept asking me again and again. I still said, "No."

After a few minutes, she asked me again, and by then, I was angry. I grew tired of listening to Veronica, again and again, asking me to go to church. After using some expletives, I agreed to go with her.

In our younger years, Veronica didn't attend church every week, but after we were married, she started going to church a little more with her mother. When she did attend church, she would always ask me to go. I always refused.

It reminded me of when Delilah repeatedly asked Samson, "Where does your strength lie?" Then Samson finally broke and told her! So, I finally agreed to go.

Going to church that day changed my life for the good forever! The pastor gave the altar call, and Veronica went to the altar and accepted Jesus into her life. As she passed in front of me, she grabbed my hand; I pushed it away. Then, her mother passed in front of me in the pew. She grabbed my hand,

and again, I pushed it away. I was watching and saw her mother crying and hugging her daughter at the altar. Then, I saw another person go up to the altar with a big smile. In front of the church, someone else went to celebrate Veronica's decision to come to Christ.

I wasn't convinced, so I stayed in the pew. I remember a gentleman tapping me on the shoulder and whispering in my ear, "I will go pray with you if you like."

I said, "I don't want to go up there."

The people in the country church looked so happy; my wife looked happy, my mother-in-law looked happy, and the pastor looked happy. Only a short time had passed, but it seemed like forever. I noticed the pastor quickly glance at me, and I guess he saw I had a cold look. He then went on to say, "Well, it has been a wonderful day, but I guess the service is over."

After he said those words, it hit me. It was then I knew I would miss out on the greatest gift anyone could experience. I prayed and said, "Lord, if you let them sing one more song, I will go to the altar."

My heart sank when the pastor said, "We are done," and started walking off the stage.

Then, he suddenly stopped, turned around, returned to the stage, and said, "I think we will sing another song. How about *Amazing Grace*?" The piano player hit the first note no sooner than I found my way to the altar and asked Christ to forgive me of my sins and come into my life. It was as if I floated to the altar even though I knew I hadn't. Little did I know how important accepting God into my life would be.

Before accepting Christ, Veronica and I were like all other couples. We had our ups and downs, but for the most part, there were good times.

Veronica and I worked hard. My wife went to beauty school, but I wasn't too fond of school, so I found work wherever possible. I was always willing to work hard and never had a problem finding jobs. My grandfather, James Arthur Copher, once told me, "A man willing to work will not have a problem finding work." He was right; guys like me were in high demand. The work was not always easy or clean, but I could always find work. Today, they call young adults, like I was, "work ready."

Veronica and I enjoyed being together. We had lots of laughs, went away on unplanned trips, stayed out late, and slept in on the weekends. We didn't go to church regularly early on, so Saturday night was our date night to go out or have friends over. We were enjoying our life, saving money, and having fun, or so we thought. We committed to not having children, fearing it would mess everything up. So, why would we want to mess our lives up by having kids?

But our plans were not always God's plans. He always redirects our path for our good. Even though we were happy, something was missing. There had to be more to life than working, traveling on the weekends, and doing the same thing repeatedly.

During the early years of our marriage, for the most part, we did not go to Sunday church services; it's funny how much church revolves around our lives today.

I first really noticed Veronica at a mutual friend's wedding. It was a smaller church than we were married in, and it was there she caught my eye. Veronica had long blonde hair, but at the wedding she had her hair cut short. I liked the new look, and I asked her out on a date. We had known each other before the wedding, but she had more interest in me than I did in her. It was a small country church where she caught my eye; our mutual friend's wedding is where I asked her out on a date.

Our first date was at Pizza Hut a couple of weeks later. We didn't go out much while dating because her mother, Virgie, who is no longer with us, wouldn't let us go out alone together. The principal place I was able to see Veronica was at a church because Virgie told me I had to go to church if I wanted to see her daughter. I wasn't big on going to church, even though my parents took me to church as a child, but I was willing to go so I could see Veronica.

Veronica and I dated for two-and-a-half years before we were married. On our date night one evening, we were on our way to Howards Mill First Church of God, which we attended with her mother. Veronica and I were riding in the back seat. I was playing with a ring she always wore on her finger. I took the ring she was wearing off and slipped an engagement ring onto her finger. The car was dark. I pointed at the ring and then asked her to marry me. She said, "Yes."

Of course, I had to ask permission from her father, Bynam (no longer with us), and after dating for a couple of years, we were married on April 7, 1983, in the church we were going to the night I proposed.

April 7, 1983, Veronica and Chris's wedding day   Veronica with her mother, Virgie Walters

Everything changed the day I asked Jesus to come into my life. I felt like I was living a new life. I had a new way of doing things and made new friends. We started going to church every Sunday, which still stands and operates today even though we no longer go there. We attended services on Sunday morning, Sunday night, Wednesday night, and other special events at that church. We loved the closeness a small country church offers.

We started traveling to gospel singing revivals, special events, and anything related to the church. Still, we were more determined than ever not to have children because we enjoyed our travels. We were away too much, going to our local and other church events.

I was happy and content, but little did I know I was really going to look back on the day I accepted Jesus and depend on Him more than ever to help my family.

Chapter 2
...To Bonds of Marriage

"Eye has not seen, nor ear heard, nor have entered into the heart of man the things which GOD has prepared for those who love HIM!"

1 CORINTHIANS 2:9

In early 1995, I was diagnosed with synovial sarcoma in my foot, and the outlook was bleak. Dr. Frank Burke, an excellent doctor, now retired, from Lexington, Kentucky, told me, "This diagnosis is life-threatening, and to save your life, you'll most likely lose your leg." He sent me to one of Cincinnati's best foot and leg doctors, Dr. James Sammarco.

During my cancer treatment, we traveled to Cincinnati three times a week, and several times, I stayed overnight in the hospital. I remember one frigid and snowy day, Veronica and I had to leave for Cincinnati early in the morning. I couldn't drive, and Veronica was uncomfortable driving in the weather, so my late father, Frank Williams, drove us to the hospital. At one point, they inserted a steel pin through my third toe to the arch of my foot for three months. It was very uncomfortable, but I learned to live with it. It was a tough time, but the Lord got us through.

When I was first diagnosed with cancer, it seemed so dark and lonely at home with Veronica and me. Uncertain of the outcome, I said goodbye to her. I told her that she was the best thing that had ever happened to me and that I loved her. She was crying, I was crying, and we hugged for the longest time and prayed together.

She looked at me and said, "You are not leaving me alone. I want a child."

Through this cancer journey, I had many surgeries. I told Veronica we would start a family, but first, "Let's get through the next surgery and off a lot of the medications."

Right before they put me under for my first surgery, I remember saying a prayer as the mask was coming down over my face. I didn't ask for the Lord to save my life; I only asked the Lord to save my leg because the doctor told me not to be surprised after surgery if my leg was gone.

In the recovery room, as I was waking up, I saw a nurse standing over me. I asked her two questions: "Do you have something for this severe headache? Do I still have my leg?"

She said yes to both as she stuck a needle filled with medicine into my thigh to relieve the headache.

There were several more trips to Cincinnati, many more hospital stays, and more surgeries. After six months of traveling, I had a clean bill of health. After my clean bill of health, they first saw me every three months, then every six months, and then once a year, and I was cancer-free, cured of this type of cancer, and no longer had to go for checkups.

The cancer diagnosis was a dark time in our lives. But God cured me of cancer, and I still had my leg. During this time, we also found out Veronica was pregnant with our first child. We were thrilled we decided to have a child. I often wonder, I don't know, maybe the cancer was God's way for us to choose to have children.

On November 3, 1996, our daughter Kristen was born. Throughout the pregnancy, I told Veronica I would not be one of those husbands who panicked when it came time for delivery. But I did. I drove too fast, took the curves way too sharply, and even ran a few stop signs and red lights. Halfway through the trip, Veronica cried out, "Slow down, you're gonna kill me."

I answered, "You are not having this baby in the car." The hospital was only 15 minutes from home, but it felt like an hour, even with my crazy driving.

When we checked into the hospital, they asked Veronica if she wanted an epidural. Veronica answered, "No! I want to have her naturally."

I leaned over to the nurse and whispered, "Get it ready."

As the pain intensified, Veronica became more unstable. Her family members were standing in the room, and at one point, she yelled, "You all get out." She grabbed my arm and twisted it until I cried out for the epidural. After she received the epidural, Veronica settled down, and it was a beautiful event for both her and me.

When her pain was managed, Veronica called out, "Tell the family to come in; let them all in." What a dramatic difference! What did women do before epidurals?

I'm old enough to remember when no one was allowed in the birthing room, especially men folk. As the birth time got closer, I remember a nurse asking me, "Do you want to be in the birthing room?"

I said to the nurse, "Let me think about it." There was still some time, so I walked back to where our family was waiting and gave them an update. On my way to chat with the family, I met a young man whose wife was about to give birth to their first child.

I asked him if he was going into the birthing room, and he reluctantly said, "Yes." As I spoke to our family, the nurse called for him and said it was time for his baby to be delivered, so he hurriedly left. I decided to go back to check on my wife, and as I walked down the hall, I saw the young man standing in the room watching the delivery of his child. The door was open, and I could see in; he suddenly passed out, and I saw a nurse leaving his wife to assist him because he was lying on the floor.

I remember saying to myself, "I'm not going into the birthing room," but I did, and I loved it. I wouldn't have missed the birth of our daughter for anything. We had a beautiful, healthy, 7-pound, 12-ounce girl named Kristen Faith Williams.

Our daughter, Kristen Hamm

We didn't want Kristen to grow up alone, so we decided to have another child. Two years and two months after she was born, Aaron Christopher Williams came into the world a healthy 9-pound, 13-ounce baby boy.

We felt our family was complete; we had one girl and one boy. Two children were enough for us. We were an average middle-class family working hard, paying our taxes, attending church, and taking vacations. There were ups and downs, mostly ups, and we happily stayed together.

In 2008, another family member came into our lives: a six-month-old girl, Hailey Anderson. She is a brilliant girl. Initially, she stayed with us on and off for several years, and when she was ten years old, she moved in with us permanently. We have been blessed to have her as a member of our family.

Aaron's kindergarten graduation

Hailey Anderson, Chris's niece

Chapter 3
From the Love of Sport...

"Lord, when doubts fill my mind, when my heart is in turmoil, quiet me and give me renewed hope and cheer."

PSALM 94:19

We are a sports family. When Kristen and Aaron were in high school, they played basketball. When they were younger, they played soccer, softball, baseball, football, and basketball. They seemed to like basketball the most and decided to stick with it as their primary sport.

Kristen played for J.B. McNabb Middle School and Montgomery County High School. Her sports career was riddled with injuries. During her sophomore year, she broke her nose in an ATV accident, and when she was a junior, she tore her ACL. After the accident, her

Kristen playing basketball, Montgomery County

sports career was pretty much over, but it was OK. She had fun playing when she was healthy, and she was able to heal quickly after her injuries. She's healthy now, and that's the main thing.

Aaron loved playing basketball; he played in middle and high school, like his sister. However, things were not working out with his high school head coach and assistant coach. There was too much going on in the school system. The superintendent wasn't the best; changes were eventually made, and he is no longer there. The coaches had boys who were preferred over others. I spoke to the coaches, but the conversation didn't go well, and I didn't like what I heard. We had a hard decision to make.

Aaron had a lot of time invested in basketball. He played basketball year-round, and he loved it. He played on AAU teams and worked with a private basketball coach, Andre McHorn. I loved watching Kristen and Aaron play ball; it was fun and relaxing, and I liked being in a gym. During these years, our lives revolved around church and basketball.

Aaron playing basketball for Bath County before his accident

Since things weren't working out at Montgomery County, I talked with Aaron about our choices: we leave Montgomery County High School, or he quit playing ball altogether. I was ready to quit. We were all discouraged, but Aaron loved playing ball. I asked him, "Aaron, do you want to quit playing ball or transfer?"

Aaron answered me, saying, "I want to transfer." Aaron played a few more games at Montgomery County High School, and then we decided to leave so he could play basketball at another school.

From the Love of Sport... 21

Aaron wasn't the only one who left the team. Right around the time Aaron left, several of the other boys either quit or transferred to other schools. Some of the boys went on to play for Clark County, some went to Bath County and Menifee County, and some stopped playing ball altogether.

The first school to reach out to us was Menifee County. They heard Aaron was leaving his current school and wanted him to come and play for them. Bath County had just hired a new basketball coach, Coach Noble, so I asked Aaron what he wanted to do. Aaron said he liked playing ball and would like to transfer to Bath County. It was a unanimous decision, so we decided to continue his basketball career in neighboring Bath County. We liked what Bath County had to offer. We liked what Coach Noble said, and we enjoyed the people. They treated us like gold.

It was a long drive to Menifee, and Veronica and I didn't want to drive on the curvy roads, and we also didn't want Aaron driving those roads. Bath County was closer than Menifee, only about 20 minutes from where we live. We thought it would be safer for Aaron and us to drive, not realizing Bath County was the road where Aaron would wreck.

My mother's side of the family was from Bath County. My grandfather and grandmother lived in a little community called Preston, Kentucky. I loved my grandparents, and I loved being on the farm. I visited and would stay with my grandparents often, and as a child, I stayed with them all summer when the school year was finished. I loved the uncomplicated way of life on the farm.

It was hard work on the farm, yet at the same time, it was simple living. We planted vegetables and cared for the fruit trees. I helped milk the cows and gather eggs from the chickens. There were hogs and cattle to care for. I have always been a hard worker and learned the value of working with my grandfather on the farm. Even though my grandfather wasn't a horse person, he allowed me to have a horse to ride. Papaw would say, "Horse eats grass down to the ground." Yet he loved me enough to have a horse. I wish my children could have had an opportunity to meet my grandparents.

The Bath County School system treated us well. The superintendent, Harvey Tackett, the counselors, principals, and teachers were fantastic. We could not have asked to be treated better. It was working out great with the basketball team, but little did we know that our family's decision to change schools would change our lives forever.

So, Aaron transferred. I wouldn't have made the same decision again, but it's too late now. If I had to do it over, we would have quit basketball altogether and stayed in Montgomery County like many of the other boys did.

It was almost time for the homecoming dance during Aaron's junior year in high school. Most high school students came up with something creative when they asked their date to go to homecoming and other dances. Aaron drew a basketball goal on a large piece of cardboard. He painted the question, "Will you go to homecoming with me?" Under the basketball goal, two baskets were hanging on the cardboard: a "Yes" basket and a "No" basket. Aaron handed a Nerf ball to the young girl and asked her if she wanted to go to the homecoming dance and put the ball into the basket: yes or no? She dropped the ball into the 'yes' basket!

Aaron asking Paige to homecoming dance

Camaro Aaron was driving to homecoming dance

Chapter 4
...To a Life-Altering Accident

"The Lord says, "I will rescue those who love me. I will protect those who trust in my name. When they call on me, I will answer; I will be with them in trouble. I will rescue them and honor them. I will satisfy them with a long life, and give them my salvation."

PSALM 91:14-16

Homecoming is an exciting time for high school students, and Aaron asked if I would let him drive my classic 1976 Camaro to the dance. The car looked great, and it wasn't hopped up, even though it had a 350 engine. I agreed he could drive, but the original plan was for me to drive the Camaro to Bath County, and then Aaron would drive through town, pick up his date, and go to the homecoming dance.

However, before the dance plans were made, Veronica and I had planned a church trip to the Cincinnati Zoo. I was one of the van drivers for the trip, so I felt obligated to go. I wanted to go on the outing and spend the day with church friends, but I didn't want Aaron driving from Montgomery County to Bath County. People took two routes from Montgomery County to Bath County High School; one was the interstate, and the other was a country road, Route 60.

I told him since I was going out of town, I didn't feel comfortable for him to drive to Bath County in an old car. Aaron told me he would be OK driving the car since he had driven it several times before. Aaron didn't like the interstate, so he drove the country road.

Aaron was a great kid. He was well-mannered and a good student. Aaron never caused Veronica or me any problems. I once told a friend, "If there ever was a perfect son, Aaron is it."

Our trip to the Cincinnati Zoo was an all-day excursion. We had left early for the zoo and planned to stay until it closed at 5:00 PM. Aaron's homecoming dance was in the evening, so he would be gone before we arrived home to take pictures at Earl and Lisa's house.

Veronica and Chris at the Cincinnati Zoo with the church group

Around 4:00 PM, I suddenly felt very uneasy, and I told Veronica, "We have to leave the zoo now." I couldn't leave the zoo fast enough.

Some group members started to gather a little early before the zoo closed, and I told them I had a very uneasy feeling and we needed to leave and get everyone gathered at the exit of the zoo. Fifty-three people from our church went on the zoo trip. The caravan consisted of three passenger vans, and a few cars followed, so it wasn't as simple as saying, "Let's go." We had to gather everybody up to leave. So, Veronica sent out a text message to the group, telling them it was time to go, that I had an uneasy feeling. The word started to spread, and our fellow travelers started to meet at the exit where Veronica and I were waiting with other members.

I was extremely nervous, and my heart was pounding, but I didn't know why. I just knew we needed to leave. I started growing agitated; I thought it was taking way too long for people to come together. All three church vans needed gas. I didn't want to stop, but we stopped for fuel and were finally on the road, returning to Winchester, our original meeting place.

The wreck happened on Saturday, September 19, 2015. The events of that day are still very real, as if they happened yesterday, even though, as I write this, the wreck was over eight years ago. My heart still breaks, and I still shed tears; this event was so traumatic for my family and me. My cancer in 1995 does not even come close to what we were about to face.

I wasn't at the crash scene, but there were two gentlemen, Larry and Daniel, on the road Aaron was driving, and their stories were the same.

Aaron was traveling along the old country road on his way to Owingsville to pick up his date for homecoming. There was a light, misty rain; while it wasn't dark, it was early evening at dusk. As he was driving on a stretch of road, his back tire slid off the side of the road. There wasn't a shoulder on the road, just a bank, and it went straight down. Aaron over-corrected when he tried to maneuver back onto the road, sending the Camaro swerving out of control and over an embankment into a tree. The car immediately burst into flames. Now my 16- year-old son lay unconscious in a destroyed, burning car close to death.

Aaron was doing everything right. He just found himself in a challenging situation a 16-year-old driver couldn't manage. Several experienced drivers may not have been able to manage the situation either. He wasn't on his cell phone or listening to the radio. We checked into that. He was not speeding. He was wearing a seatbelt. He had it buckled. We know this because the seatbelt coupling was locked in the holder, and the flames were so hot and close to him that they burned the seatbelt into it.

Larry, one of the gentlemen traveling along the highway in front of Aaron, said, "I kept watching him in my rear-view mirror because I liked old cars." He later said, "I know your son wasn't driving fast because I was driving 50 MPH, and he was well behind me."

Daniel Richmond with Aaron

Larry Carper helped pull Aaron out of the car

Daniel the second gentleman's story, is the same as Larry's version. He was checking on a private farm not too far from the crash site. It was a piece of property where he and his fiancé were going to be married. When Daniel arrived at the venue, he had forgotten the key to the farm gate, so he turned around and left to go back and get the key. That was the providence of God protecting Aaron, I do believe.

Daniel was coming down the road in the opposite direction as he passed Larry. Then he saw Aaron driving the Camaro and losing control of the car, going side to side. Daniel tried to move over, thinking Aaron would come across the road and hit him head-on, but Aaron went down a bank and hit a tree, and Daniel saw flames coming up from the bank.

Daniel was the first person at the scene; he stopped, parked his car, and rushed down the hill. Daniel broke the door glass and saw Aaron was unconscious. Daniel told Aaron, not knowing he could not hear him, "You will not burn alone." I knew this was a remarkable feat. Aaron is 6 feet 4 inches, and a Camaro door glass is narrow.

Daniel started pulling Aaron from the wreck; the flames were so hot they burned the hair off Daniel's arm. As he pulled Aaron halfway out of the Camaro, he noticed a large piece of metal fall from the back of Aaron's head. Daniel said the flames were so hot he didn't take the time to see what it was, but blood started pouring out of Aaron's head. Daniel had him halfway out of the car when Larry came running down the hill to help. The two of them managed to get Aaron out of the car. Daniel cradled him up in his arms and started up the hillside. When they were halfway up the hill carrying Aaron, the car blew up.

My son would have had no chance if it weren't for these two brave individuals. By then, a couple of other cars had stopped; one was a young lady, Denise, and her husband, Terry Barnett. Aaron was now lying on the tailgate of a truck. Denise said, "This boy doesn't stand a chance if we don't stop the bleeding." She grabbed a towel and applied pressure. Those around heard Aaron take one big breath, and then Denise said, "We just lost him. He isn't breathing."

About the time Aaron took that last breath, the ambulance came down the road, and it must have startled him because he shook. They said he started breathing again. I believe, once again, God sent that ambulance on time, and I believe the Lord sent Daniel to go back for his key. I believe this was all God's doing.

People have told me Aaron was sure lucky, and I always say, "I believe it was the Lord."

At 6:38 PM, about halfway through our trip home from the Cincinnati Zoo, Veronica received a call from Claudette Faudere, the mother of the young lady Aaron was on his way to pick up for the dance. Veronica was in the back seat, talking to friends, relaxing from our day trip to the zoo. When the phone rang, and she saw who it was, she thought Claudette was calling to see how close we were and if we were going to make it back before the pictures were taken.

Veronica excitedly answered the phone, "Hello!"

But Claudette immediately told Veronica how Aaron had been in an accident. Veronica asked, "Well, how bad is he?"

Ambulance and firetrucks at the accident scene

Claudette said, "It's really bad. I heard they were going to airlift him to the University of Kentucky Hospital (UK Hospital)."

While Veronica was talking with Claudette, Earl, a good friend of mine, called me. His son was in Aaron's class at school and played on the basketball team with him. Earl's home was where they were all meeting to take pictures. He told me Aaron was in a car wreck.

Veronica, riding in the back seat, started talking louder and louder. She started to get my attention because she was talking so loudly. I wanted her to quiet down a little so I could hear Earl on the phone. I knew she was getting upset, and I knew this couldn't be good. When I was able to hear Earl, he told me the same thing: Aaron was in a car wreck. Then I asked Earl, "How bad is it?"

Earl said, "I am headed down there now, but I hear it's really bad."

We live in a small town, but Owingsville in Bath County is smaller than Mt. Sterling, so news travels fast. When Larry and Daniel pulled Aaron out of the car, his phone fell to the ground, and another man who stopped, Brock Baber, saw Aaron's phone and picked it up. He started trying to go through it to call somebody. The last text to Aaron was from Paige, the girl he was picking up for the dance. Brock called her, and that's how she found out what happened. Her mother immediately called Veronica, so Veronica found out from Claudette before the ambulance even got to Aaron.

The hospital in Mt. Sterling was closest to Aaron's accident, but they wanted to airlift Aaron to the University of Kentucky Hospital in Lexington. However, the mist from the rain made it too dangerous to go directly to UK Hospital, so they first took him to Saint Joseph's Hospital in Mt. Sterling.

The hospital in Mt. Sterling wasn't equipped to handle injuries as serious as Aaron's brain trauma. It was in Saint Joseph's emergency room that Veronica's sister entered the room with tears running down her face. She started screaming Aaron's name, "Wake up!"

My cousin, one of the nurses at the hospital, grabbed her arm and looked at her, shaking her head as if to say, "He can't hear you. He's not going to make it."

I want to be clear here: we attend a great church. It's what church should be about. Today, Veronica and I still attend the same church, the Epperson First Church of God in Clark County. After we received news of the accident, the gentleman sitting in the passenger seat told me to pull over. Everyone in our van moved to the other two vans and other cars so Veronica and I could take the one van directly to the hospital. At the time, Veronica, and I... I don't know how to describe it; I guess we were in shock. We just knew we needed to get there NOW!

Veronica and I headed straight to the University of Kentucky Hospital because we were told he would end up there. We arrived at the UK Hospital before Aaron and the ambulance, not knowing what we would find. As time elapsed, our anticipation grew. The entire time we were waiting I thought I would be able to talk to my son when he arrived. You hear about car wrecks all the time. They will check him out and send us home. Things just don't happen to normal people in a bad way.

Veronica was inside the waiting room, trying to find out what she could. I was standing at the entrance to the ER, where they brought the patients in by ambulance. The hospital was a hectic place, being a Saturday evening in Lexington. Every time an ambulance pulled up, I thought it was our son, but it wasn't.

After what felt like an eternity, another ambulance came, and I knew Aaron was on this one. The door swung open, and a female EMS worker was at the door. I knew I surprised her because I was standing right at the opening of the door's entrance to the ambulance.

I asked her, "Is that boy alive?"

She said, "Yes, barely," and they quickly moved him inside. They had the stretcher moving so quickly, so I couldn't touch him; I just wanted to touch him. I did keep trying to talk to him, but there was no response. She told me, "He can't hear you."

I never went into the hospital; I don't know why I just didn't. I don't know how much time passed. Finally, one lone doctor came out and told me, "Your son has a severe Diffuse Axonal Traumatic Brain Injury. In layman's terms, his brain has been decapitated from his body, and all his neurons are spinning in his head, and he won't live through the night."

In short, I responded, "You mean to tell me that boy will not live through the night?"

"I am sorry," the doctor said.

Veronica and I came together in shock, and we just hugged one another in disbelief. Behind the scenes, a team of doctors and a couple of nurses discussed Aaron's condition. We knew one of the nurses, and when we saw her a few weeks later, she told us they were discussing the passing of Aaron. She told the team of doctors, "When he does pass, I will go to the parents since I know them."

A few minutes later, two doctors came outside. They told me if Aaron were going to have any chance, they would have to drill a hole into his skull. The pressure was building on his brain. I stood there for a minute thinking; I couldn't believe this was happening. I wasn't thinking about what they just said. I was standing there in disbelief. The day had started like other days; it was a good day. The weather was beautiful, we had the trip to the zoo, Aaron was going to the homecoming dance, and now it had ended with this nightmare. The doctor snapped me back to reality and said, "Mr. Williams, you need to make a decision; he has no chance without it. We need to relieve the pressure off his brain."

I asked him, "If this was your son, what would you do?"

He said, "I would do it without a doubt."

So, I signed the papers.

When they took us back to the emergency room, the doctor talked to us, telling us in medical terms what was wrong with Aaron. We did not know what Diffuse Axonal Traumatic Brain Injury was, but the doctor outside the emergency room put it in simpler terms.

We walked out, and they took him straight to surgery.

After the two doctors spoke with me about drilling a hole in his skull and I signed the permission papers, I sat on the curb outside the emergency room and began to pray. I prayed for the Lord to save my son. That's all I said. "Lord, save my son." I didn't know what else to say. There was a lot of movement outside the emergency room. A Saturday night in Lexington, KY, had a lot happening, but I didn't care who saw me or heard me. I knew my son was in critical condition, and all I could do was pray for him. I prayed to God, who was the only one who could help him.

But I was not the first to pray.

My church family in the van prayed on their way back from the zoo trip.

Back at the crash site, there was a prayer group. Brock Baber, the gentleman at the accident who found Aaron's phone, told the group of people, "We need to pray for this young man, for he is in serious condition." Brock and the others began praying for Aaron's life.

Everything that worked out was because of the Lord. When they brought him into Mt. Sterling Hospital, I believe it was a blessing from God because they couldn't immediately fly him out to UK. It was raining, so they had to stop at Mt. Sterling Hospital, and they were able to perform some procedures to help him. I believe they also may have been able to do intervention in the ambulance as well.

When they brought him to the emergency room at St. Joseph's in Mt. Sterling, one of the nurses we've grown to love told us when Aaron came into the emergency room, she knew there was something so different about him. Even though they knew he was close to death, you could feel the presence of God. She said, "I know we are not supposed to, but we need to pray for this young man." They joined hands, and she led them in prayer.

Brock Baber, first person to pray at the accident site and also contacted Paige's mom

Back in Owingsville, the people at the homecoming dance were praying; a deep sadness filled the gym. The principal, Sean Bailey, was also the pastor of a Christian Church in town, and he asked if anyone wanted to join him in his church for prayer. He took teachers and students to his church, and they began to pray for my son. The church was full.

There was a lot of prayer going on before I said my prayer on the curb outside of the emergency room at UK Hospital. Little did I know these prayers were just a drop in the ocean for what was about to come. Prayers came from all over the world.

Prayer vigil for Aaron

Chapter 5
The First Night From Life-Saving Care...

"For God so loved the world, that He gave His only Son, that whoever believes in Him should not perish but have eternal life."

JOHN 3:16 NKJV

When I was Aaron's age, I drove a 1970 Camaro, and later I drove a 1976 Camaro, the same model Aaron was driving the night of his accident. There were several times I went to race at the Clay City Drag Strip. Also, I did some stunts on the county roads.

There was another public road on Paris Pike. It had a long straight stretch, and we would go there to drag race. You could see miles down the road and many times we would line up at the top of the hill and reach speeds over 100 MPH. It was called the Paris Pike Drag Strip. My old cars were hopped up, so they would go fast. I worked on them constantly with a friend of mine, Jeff Yarber.

Another road, Stepstone-Robertson Road, was a place where teenage boys would go to jump their cars. The road had three big humps, and a bunch of us boys would go to see how many humps we could fly over airborne. Sometimes we'd go over one hump, other times two, and one night I went airborne over all three humps like on *Dukes of Hazzard*. When I went airborne, I was so afraid and wished I hadn't done it, but it was too late. When I landed, I hit the pavement, broke the shocks, knocked my bumper off, and damaged the muffler, and I lived to talk about it. I used to do all kinds of crazy stuff in that Camaro, and sometimes, I wasn't physically able to drive.

When I was younger, I drove my car fast; Aaron was 16 and never drove fast. I was a reckless driver, often going well over 100 MPH; Aaron was only driving 50 when he wrecked his car. I was never angry at God over Aaron's wrecking, but I did ask God why. I asked God why Aaron wrecked when he was doing everything right, and I never wrecked, and I did everything wrong. I asked God why when I prayed daily for my children's safety when they drove. Why did God let this happen? Why wasn't God with him that night?

The Lord spoke to my heart, not in a voice we hear out loud, but the voice of the Holy Spirit to my heart.

"I was with him when Daniel forgot the key to the gate.

"I was with him when someone knew to apply pressure to the back of his head.

"I was with him when the ambulance came down the road and startled him.

"I was with him when Brock stopped by to pray.

"I was with him when they couldn't fly him out and took him to Saint Joseph.

"And I am with him now."

After hearing God's answer that first night, I never asked God why again. And a scripture passage I had never thought of before came to my mind:

1 Peter 4:12-13: "Beloved, do not think it's strange concerning the fiery trails which is to try you, as though some strange thing happened to you but rejoice inasmuch as you partake of Christ suffering when His glory shall be revealed, you may be glad also with exceeding joy."

The night of Aaron's accident, the doctors feared the worst, but they never stopped trying to save Aaron's life. I am so thankful to them for not giving up on him. I couldn't have asked for a better team of doctors and nurses. God was really with him at the crash site, St. Joe's in Mount Sterling, and UK Hospital.

Aaron was alive but on life support. He was in critical condition in the ICU brain trauma unit on the 6th floor of UK Hospital. He had a 3-inch cut on the back of his head into his skull close to his brain, concussion, fracture to the skull by his eye socket, broken collarbone, broken ribs, bruised lung, kidney damage, and brain injury called a Diffuse Axonal Injury (DAI). He had no brain waves; he had a feeding tube, a trachea, and a tube in his skull to relieve the pressure around his brain.

The doctors at UK Hospital weren't as concerned about the broken bones; their primary focus was on Aaron's brain injury. They told Veronica and me they use a scale to measure brain injuries: a score of 0, you were dead; 1 to 3, you were awfully close to death. When patients have a score of 4 to 6, there is hope. Patients who scored 7 to 10 will most likely live but will live with physical and possible mental handicaps for the rest of their lives; however, there was a good chance they'd survive.

Aaron measured a 1.0.

The night Aaron arrived in the ICU, over 200 people from across Montgomery, Bath, and Powell counties came to visit with us. The nurses allowed all 200 hundred people in, four at one time, to see Aaron, and they could only stay for a couple of minutes. Later, we found out the reason they let visitors come. They were sure he would not live through the night, and the nursing staff wanted family and friends to see him for the last time when he was alive.

Throughout the night, Veronica and I would leave Aaron's room and say hello to Aaron's many visitors, but we wanted to get back to Aaron as soon as possible. The people stayed all night in the waiting room. Veronica and I would step out of Aaron's room to take a break and talk with people who were there for the night.

While we were sitting in the ICU unit with Aaron, a nurse came in and told us a couple of local TV news stations, WLEX 18 and WKYT 27, had come. The reporters asked if they could interview us. We agreed and went downstairs, outside the hospital,

Prayer service for Aaron

36 From Death to Life

News anchor Amber Philpot WKYT

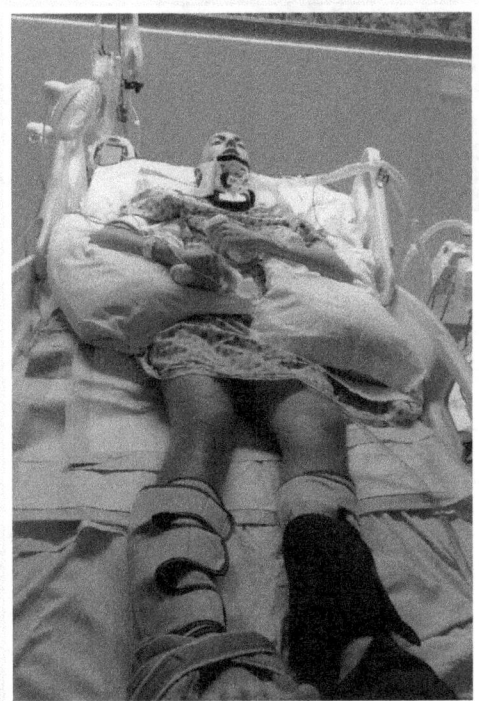
Aaron in a coma at UK Hospital

and we did the interview. After the interview aired, the story was all over Central and Eastern Kentucky.

The waiting room stayed full for days; the people just didn't go home. Day 1, full. Day 2, full. Day 3, full. After the airing on the news stations, more and more people we didn't know were coming. There was no official head count, but there were two to three hundred people each night. They supported us with food, anointed cloths, anointed blankets, and money. Most of all, they were united in PRAYER. The support from all our friends and family was unbelievable.

Aaron was in a coma and was now in the hands of the Lord and good doctors. The worst nightmare my wife and I had ever experienced was the first 24 hours after the accident. I don't wish this nightmare on anyone. They told us he didn't have much chance to survive the night, but he did! Aaron's long journey of healing was just beginning.

"Pray for Aaron" signs posted in many yards

Chapter 6
...To Prayers Around the World

> "Now God worked unusual miracles by the hands of Paul, so that even handkerchiefs or aprons were brought from his body to the sick, and the diseases left them, and the evil spirits went out of them."
>
> ACTS 19:11-12

I can't tell you the number of times throughout Aaron's hospital stay when the local news teams, WLEX 18 and WKYT 27, came and asked for interviews. We'd go downstairs through the lobby to the outside and provide updates. After a couple of days and TV interviews, people from around the state came to support us and Aaron. Aaron was in critical condition, still at stage 1, but he was alive. I remember people's outpouring of concern and the prayers we received over the next few days.

I don't know how many pastors called their congregations to pray for Aaron. I have countless photos of people praying at Church gatherings: large churches, country churches, and churches of all sizes, people gathering at the altar and praying for my son. Some churches had people two rows deep kneeling at the altar; some had ten people, and in other churches, there were people ten rows deep at the altar. I can't remember the number of pictures sent to us, but I know they encouraged us. What always surprised me was the number of faithful people who prayed and did not even know Aaron.

We were surrounded by much more than prayer at church; we received an outpouring of support during our stay in the hospital and throughout our local communities. Every day, somebody different would come and ask to pray for Aaron. During this time, since Aaron was in such a critical condition, people couldn't just ring the bell at the nurses' station and come back to visit Aaron. They needed permission from us to come back. Whenever someone came, I would only ask one question: "Has God told you to come and pray for my son?"

When people answered "YES," I would allow them to come back.

Some visitors preferred not to go to Aaron's room, so they prayed in the waiting room. They didn't want to see him that way. Once again, people gave us prayer cloths, and others would join our hands for prayer. I knew that prayer was the one thing to get Aaron out of this mess.

I remember one time; it just seemed so dark, and it may have been because we didn't see a lot of improvement. One of the nurses came into the room and said a couple of ladies were asking to speak with us. I went out to the ICU waiting room and pushed the doors open. I saw these two ladies standing there, with long hair and long dresses, holding onto their bibles.

"Can I help you ladies?" I asked.

"You are Aaron's father; we saw you on the news. We have come to pray for your son," they responded.

"Where did you come from?" I asked.

They replied, "Manchester, Kentucky."

"You mean to tell me you drove all the way from Manchester just to pray for Aaron? Is there any other reason you came to Lexington? There are good shopping and eating places."

They gently responded, "We came to Lexington only to have prayer with Aaron."

Manchester, Kentucky is about two hours away in the Eastern part of State. I said, "Let's do it."

Knowing their faith or, I thought I did, I knew they could be a little vocal, and everything had to be quiet in the ICU. I suggested we go to the waiting room for a big throw-down prayer session.

When I suggested this, one of the ladies said, "No, we want to lay hands on your son."

"Do you think God has told you to lay hands on my son?"

"Yes."

I said, "Keep it down, and come on in."

I didn't care what faith you were if you were a good Christian; I just needed prayers for my son. The two ladies came in and laid their hands on Aaron; they said powerful and beautiful prayers. They went home after praying, and I never saw them again.

A couple of days later, an elderly Black lady stood near the ICU unit door. She asked the nurse if she could speak with me. Of course, I agreed. I didn't care if you were white, black, brown, or green; we are all God's children, and if you took the time to come and pray for Aaron, I was surely going to allow you to do just that. So, I went to the ICU doors and asked, "Can I help you?"

She said, "I have driven from the other side of Lexington to pray for your son."

So, I asked her if she wanted to come back to pray over Aaron. She said, "We can pray in the waiting room."

"OK, let's do it."

After every sentence, she would say, "In the name of Jesus." This was her prayer:

"Be with Aaron's parents, in the name of Jesus.

"Be with the nurses, in the name of Jesus.

"Be with the doctors, in the name of Jesus."

Her prayer went on for 20 minutes or more. At one point, I thought she had finished praying, so I tried to stand up, but she wasn't done. She grabbed my hand and gently pulled me back down. I don't know how she thought of so many things to pray about, but I know she gets it. It is truly all about Jesus.

As she finished her prayer, she said, "In the blessed name of Jesus," and she was through. I gave her a big hug, and she was gone. She is another person I have never seen again, and I never knew her name.

Lisa Rogers, a good friend from Bath County whose son had played ball with Aaron since they could dribble a basketball, came to the hospital. She said, "You may think this is crazy, but I brought communion, and I would like you to take it with your family when you all come together."

I told her nothing was surprising because the Lord works in mysterious ways. So, when our family came together – my brother, mother, daughter,

Lisa Rogers brought communion to the hospital for the Williams' family

wife, and me – we all gathered around Aaron's bed, prayed, and took communion. I will never forget that moment.

Another gentleman came to Aaron's room, and like so many, I didn't have a clue as to who he was. He was a Black gentleman with long hair, wore wild, colorful clothes, and didn't say anything to us. He wandered around the room, touching everything, I mean everything, and he was praying softly. After about ten minutes, he left; we never spoke to him, but it was a great prayer.

But there is one young lady I will never forget. One day, when I stepped out of Aaron's room for a minute for a change of scenery, I went to the waiting room. A mother was walking with a young lady who was wearing hospital clothes and hooked up to an IV. She had bruises and many scratches, and they were strolling down the hall.

This young lady was driving down the bypass in Mt. Sterling. I don't remember what happened, but there was a wreck, her boyfriend died, and she was seriously injured, so the medics brought her here to UK Hospital. The young lady must have recognized me because she approached me and asked if she could see Aaron.

I told her she could, so we went to Aaron's room, and she started to cry. I don't know if it brought back memories of her wreck or what. I didn't ask. I just hugged her and said, "I will pray for you."

She said, "Thanks. I just wanted to see Aaron."

Throughout our stay at UK Hospital, other families were in the waiting room. There were five different families, each with three or four people staying with them. Like us, families and friends remained through the nights hoping for good news, but we had so many people I often wondered what they thought about the support Aaron received. I often felt sorry for them because they didn't have the people to support them.

One day, two ladies whose sons were older than Aaron but played basketball with him at Montgomery County brought food to the hospital. They brought us so much food there was enough for the other families who had loved ones in the ICU. I asked them to help themselves, and they were so thankful for having a plate of a home-cooked meal. I will never forget the ladies who brought the gift of all the food that fed so many.

The principal and superintendent of Bath County School and several parents from Bath and Montgomery counties came to support us. Bath County School had assigned parking places, and students decorated Aaron's spot with prayer requests, well wishes, and candles.

One gentleman brought 20 basketballs signed by students and posters that people had made and signed. I framed a lot of those posters, and I still have them today, along with all the basketballs. A local flower shop owner decorated the tree, which had burnt after Aaron hit it. She made an ugly sight beautiful. The young lady Aaron was to pick up for the homecoming dance, went to the crash, found his bow tie and a couple of other items, and put them in a shadow box.

Aaron's parking spot at school and all the kids signed it

Aaron was in the brain trauma unit for 12 of the 45 days he was in the hospital; Veronica took daily notes. She wrote about the good and the bad days. She knew who came to visit, and who came and prayed. She read the scriptures and played K-LOVE on the radio. Aaron moved to level 3, which was still better than a 1; however, he was still critical.

Veronica and Aaron with Bath County Superintendent, Harvey Tackett

Veronica and I started taking shifts to stay with Aaron. I stayed with him during the day, and Veronica stayed at night. We had a daughter at home who needed us as well. Aaron was holding his own at level 3. Besides all the conditions he had from the crash, Aaron developed a fever of 104 degrees and double pneumonia, which was profoundly serious and life-threatening. Aaron's condition was bad.

Nurse Megan Howard's badge   Nurse Rebecca Cooksey-Stauber's badge

During Aaron's time at UK Hospital, we had an excellent team of nurses: Megan and Rebecca. We had other nurses caring for Aaron, but those two stand out in my mind. Megan always had a cheerful outlook and encouraged us. Rebecca was more business-like.

Every day, Nurse Rebecca came into the room, shook Aaron on his shoulder, and said, "Aaron, you're in a hospital. You have been in a car wreck; give me a thumbs-up." Nothing. Aaron continued to lay there with no response.

Nurse Megan offered the encouraging words we needed so desperately. Veronica and I prayed desperately for Aaron to give a thumbs-up. He didn't give us a thumbs-up, but we were beginning to wonder if he was still alive because he was on life support.

Looking back at my cancer diagnosis years ago, we both learned a little about how to talk with doctors and nurses. At first, our question was, "How long do I have to live?" And we asked those questions about Aaron. And then, as time elapsed and we weren't seeing any improvement, we began asking different questions. You start asking more questions, "Am I going to die? How long do I have?" We were asking the same about Aaron

One of the nurses who took care of Aaron

Rebecca Cooksey-Stauber and Aaron

Throughout our stay, the people never gave up on Aaron. They kept coming. Small groups of people would hold hands and pray for Aaron. Pastors, church leaders, and ball teams came from Powell, Clark, Montgomery and Bath counties, and Lexington. So many people I didn't know came, but everyone was very welcome to pray for Aaron. He was still alive; however, in a critical condition. The people still had hope, and I knew with each passing day we still had Aaron.

The first place I went when I arrived at the hospital each day was to go to the chapel and pray. Even though I desperately wanted to see how Aaron was doing and hear any

Nurse Megan Howard and Aaron

updates from my wife, I felt it was important to be alone with the Lord. The chapel was quiet, and I never saw anyone there. It was beautiful; it looked like a small church. A bible and a kneeling bench were in front of a large cross, a pew, and a stained-glass window. It was a quiet place to pray to God—He who could change things. There were days I prayed longer than others, but every day, I prayed. After visiting the chapel for prayer, I went to see Aaron on the 6th floor and caught up on the news, but I prayed first.

One evening after leaving Veronica, I walked through the breezeway on the second floor, overlooking the lobby downstairs. I saw a group of 25 or more people passing out candles. Somehow, I knew they were here to pray for Aaron, so I decided to go downstairs and join them. I took a candle and asked them, "Who are we praying for?"

The person passing out the candles said, "There is a boy in the ICU with a brain injury named Aaron Williams." I asked if I could join them, but I didn't tell them I was Aaron's father. She said, "The more, the better." So, we all went outside, lit our candles, and had a very spiritual prayer time.

Psalm 46:1-2 was one of the scriptures read before we prayed: "God is our refuge and strength, an ever-present help in trouble. Therefore, we will not fear, though the earth gives way, and the mountains fall into the heart of the sea."

Aaron was still at level 3 on the brain damage scale, so everyone who wanted to visit still had to check with the nurse to see if they could speak to us. One evening, Veronica and I were about to make our shift change and were going over our notes and events from the day. Our backs turned toward Aaron's ICU room door when suddenly, someone asked, "Is this Aaron Williams's room?"

My first reaction was to ask, "How did you get in here?"

He said, "Oh, I just walked in and am here to pray for Aaron."

Even though I wondered how he got in, I said, "That'd be great."

Aaron had prayers from so many, but it was different this time. Before the man left, he said something to us. As he was walking out the door, he turned around and said, "Your son has been chosen."

"What do you mean my son has been chosen?" I asked.

With a smile, he said, "Time will tell," and then he was gone.

After this man's visit, it wasn't long before Aaron's condition began to improve. His brain trauma level ticked up to 4. Veronica and I were so happy Aaron had improved. I am not saying this man was a *Heavenly Visitor*, but it was strange.

Not all visitors were heavenly and positive visitors. Veronica remained with Aaron during the night when there were fewer visitors, especially after nine o'clock. One morning, Veronica shared a story with me about what happened the night before saying how last night's visitor was different.

Around 2:30 AM, Veronica was praying, reading scriptures, and listening to K-LOVE when a team of doctors came in to check on Aaron. Aaron was at a level 4, and even though Aaron had not given us a "thumbs-up" and was still on life support, the doctors gave us signs of hope.

When the doctors left, Veronica laid her head down on Aaron's chest and started praying again. She felt a presence in the room; thinking the doctors had returned, she raised her head, but it wasn't the doctors; it was a tall, dark shadow. At the time, Veronica didn't know who or what it was, but a shadow was standing there, just like the doctors were still standing there.

But then it came to her. The shadowy visitor was here to wage spiritual warfare and claim Aaron's life. She rebuked the shadow in the name of Jesus, and after a few minutes, the shadow was gone. I'm not one to believe things like what she was describing, and I was very skeptical until I found out what happened next. She said all the machines hooked up to Aaron went off; alarms started ringing, medical devices began beeping, and noise filled the room to alert Aaron's medical team. The nurses and staff came running into the room and did what they could to save Aaron's life.

Hearing Veronica retell this harrowing story reminded me of Psalm 23, Verse 4: Even though I walk through the valley of the shadow of death, I will fear no evil, for thou art with me, thy rod and thy staff comfort me.

I always hear this verse at funerals; however, it is not an end-of-life but a middle-of-life verse. Throughout his life, David often faced death. There are times during our lives we often face death: car wrecks, cancer, heart attacks, and near misses. We have all encountered situations where the shadow of death was hovering over us, and maybe we should have died. We can't always see the shadowy figure, but David must have. Veronica indeed saw it. I know there must be others who have seen it. But the shadow of death comes; for many, God chases him away and gives us more time on this earth.

Aaron survived that frightful night but wasn't out of the woods. When I arrived at the hospital one morning, the nurse said, "I don't know who or how you can reach people, but visitors cannot visit today. Aaron's condition is extremely critical; his brain trauma level fell back to a 1."

We were heartbroken. I called two good friends, one in Montgomery County and another in Bath County, and told them to spread the word for people to pray for Aaron. "I don't know how, but please get the word out; no visitors today." Once again, the people responded, and prayers rang out, but nobody came to the hospital.

A couple of days later, Aaron again showed signs of improving, but it was still overly concerning. He was still in a coma and wasn't giving us a "thumbs-up." The doctors and nurses were looking for a sign Aaron had brain activity and could respond to the words "give us a thumbs-up." Once again, his level rose to 3, but his lack of movement concerned the doctors and us.

Still, the visitors started coming again; you just couldn't keep them away, and we didn't want them to stop coming. One night, a nurse asked me if I knew what was happening in the waiting room. I said, "No." She said, "You might want to take a look."

What I saw in the waiting room shocked me. The waiting room was large, and people filled the room and spilled over down two hallways with smaller groups holding hands and praying. I don't know the number of people who came to pray. I never spoke to anyone, but they were deep in prayer and didn't even notice me. Tears filled my eyes as I watched and cried, and I eventually went back into Aaron's ICU room.

On another day, a couple asked if they could come in and see Aaron. It was Daniel Richmond, the gentleman who pulled Aaron out of the burning car at the crash site, and his wife, Megan. When I saw them, I noticed what a good-looking couple they were. After spending time with them, we hugged and thanked them, and they left. We are forever thankful to Daniel and were glad to meet his wife. We are truly blessed to know them. Because of Daniel's actions on the day of the accident, our son is still alive. To this day, we still see

Daniel Richmond with Aaron at fundraiser

them in town quite a bit.

The heroes at the accident site were affected by the trauma of the accident in their own ways. I spoke with Daniel's brother-in-law, Tracy, about Daniel pulling Aaron out of the burning car. He said Daniel and Megan came over to eat at their house the very night of the wreck, and Daniel never said one word about what had happened. Sometime later, we met Larry Carper at my wife's hair salon, Veronica's Hair Design. Larry told us he couldn't sleep for over a month because of the events that unfolded at the crash site.

I told Veronica God had taken hold of Aaron's story and blown it out worldwide. I could share different stories and interactions about the love we felt, the prayers we heard, and the community support we witnessed. Every person we interacted with during this time holds a special place in our hearts.

Every evening when I returned home, I checked my emails, no matter how exhausted I felt. I'd open my computer, and there would be one hundred or two hundred, sometimes even three thousand emails from around the world. I read every email and responded to those I could. One evening, I arrived home, and I found five thousand emails with words of encouragement, words of other people's stories of brain injuries, and prayers from across the United States and from around the world. One email was written in Japanese, and when translated, it read, "Japan is praying for Aaron Williams." The words brought tears to my eyes. I don't know how people heard about Aaron's accident and his condition or how they found my email address; it had to be a God thing.

Veronica would stop by Starbucks on her way to the hospital and a young lady working there asked, "Are you Aaron Williams' mother? I have seen you on TV."

"Yes," Veronica told her.

The lady asked Veronica if she could come back in a couple of days because she said she wanted to make her something. Veronica said, "Sure, I come every day."

After two or three days, the young lady handed Veronica a homemade blanket with scriptures written all over it. She asked if we would lay it over Aaron, and we did.

We never turned away anything referencing God. Several people sent us anointed prayer cloths, and we pinned all of them to his pillow. He slept under an anointed prayer blanket one of the churches brought us. We received prayers from all kinds of faith communities: Jewish, Catholic, Baptist, Presbyterian, and Methodist, as well as the Christian Church, the Church of Christ, and the Church of God. So many faiths shared their prayers, and we welcomed them all. We believe there is power in prayer.

I asked one of Aaron's visitors what was happening in Mt. Sterling. They responded, "Aaron Williams is what's happening in Mt. Sterling and the county; we are behind Aaron Williams." Yard signs and banners were hanging around town and on bypasses in the country. Instead of restaurant signs advertising food, they said, "Pray for Aaron," church marquees wrote "Pray for Aaron," and schools posted "Pray for Aaron."

Sunday became a day to worship God and pray for Aaron. Family, friends, and well-wishers gathered around our home; Fifty or more stood outside Aaron's bedroom, they placed a cross, sang songs, and prayed.

Prayer vigil for Aaron

The local community stepped up in so many ways. The Camaro Aaron was driving the night of the accident was yellow with a black stripe. Someone proposed a fundraiser selling yellow and black T-shirts. The design was two black stripes on the front of a yellow t-shirt and his basketball number printed on the back. AccuSigns made the T-shirts and didn't charge a dime. People near and far purchased shirts; five thousand-plus T-shirts were sold. Everybody was wearing Aaron Williams' T-shirts. We received pictures from factory workers, doctors' offices, car auctions, and schools; people in their favorite shopping places were wearing them.

Schools across the region started all their school sports games with a prayer. The fans were wearing the T-shirts. One of the Montgomery County soccer games stands out in my mind. Hundreds of people were in attendance, lined up shoulder to shoulder around the football field. The people stood beside each other, holding hands, and praying for Aaron. Bath County High School did something similar where they released balloons. Powell County High School sent pictures of the students wearing the T-shirts on the bleachers. Our community and

Kim Dice, Veronica's niece, raised money for us

Aaron with Stephanie McCarty who raised money for us

Bath County football team releasing balloons for Aaron

Soccer game at Montgomery County circling the field praying for Aaron

Powell County School wearing black to support Aaron

schools were all unified for Aaron Williams.

We met a grandmother whose granddaughter's favorite colors were yellow and black. She was making a quilt for her, and her granddaughter suddenly passed away. Maybe it was a car wreck, I don't know, but her grandmother never had the opportunity to give her the quilt. She heard about Aaron and the yellow and black T-shirt and brought Aaron the quilt she had made for her granddaughter. This is a gift we will always cherish.

Yes, Aaron Williams was what was going on in Mt. Sterling.

One morning after I arrived at the hospital and before Veronica headed home, we could sense something was different. More doctors and nurses were checking Aaron, and there were more reading monitors. Veronica and I knew and could feel a change; something was about to happen. We believed that was the day we would have to make a decision regarding Aaron's life.

Bath County High School wearing Aaron's yellow T-shirts

Yard sign posted in Bath County

Nurse Rebecca came into the room and said something different this time. Before, when she entered the room, she would say, "Aaron, you were in a car wreck. You are in a hospital. Give me a thumbs-up." She'd also shake him on the shoulder, but nothing would happen.

On this day, she came in and pressed hard on his broken collarbone. Her voice was louder than usual, "Aaron, you have been in a car wreck. You are in a hospital. I need you to give me a thumbs-up."

I noticed the words she said, "I **need** you to give me a thumbs-up."

Suddenly, Aaron finally gave a thumbs-up!

"I knew you were in there!" Rebecca told him and went running out of the room.

Veronica and I hugged and cried. I believe God intervened that morning. It reminded me of the story in the bible where Abraham was to sacrifice Isaac, his son. As Abraham obeyed the Lord and raised his knife, an angel said, "Do not lay a hand on the boy. Do not do anything to harm him. Now I know that you fear God because you have not withheld him from me, your son, your only son." Genesis 22:12.

A team of doctors came in with Rebecca and repeated what Rebecca did daily. They said, "Aaron, you've been in a car wreck. "You are in a hospital," and they would shake him on the shoulder, but Aaron did nothing.

Rebecca spoke up, "He did it! I saw him."

The doctors told her they believed her. They left the room. Veronica, me, and Aaron were the only people left.

After hundreds of visitors and thousands of prayers when Aaron was in a coma, he gave the *"thumbs-up sign,"* and it was then we knew we had a fighting chance. Aaron was in a coma for a total of 45 days; for 12 of those days, he was on the 6th floor in the ICU brain trauma unit.

After giving the thumbs-up signal, plans were in place to send Aaron to the brain trauma unit at Cardinal Hill Rehabilitation Hospital. Before leaving UK Hospital, Veronica and I had a meeting with the doctors on Aaron's team, and they told us Aaron would be handicapped for the rest of his life. They also told us to prepare our home for handicap accessibility.

Once again, as we did before, we put our trust in God no matter what the doctors told us. I believe in good doctors, and I am thankful for them because we need good men and women doctors, but no matter what they told us, our trust was in God.

Chapter 7
From Relearning Life's Basic Skills...

"Truly I tell you, if you have faith as small as a mustard seed, you can say to this mountain, 'move from here to there,' and it will move. Nothing will be impossible for you."

MATTHEW 17:20

Everything that had happened and was happening at UK Hospital was a blur to me: so many people, doctors in and out, nurses keeping watch, people sending pictures, prayer vigils, and interviews. I can't remember everything that went on at the hospital. Veronica was better at capturing those moments at the time than I was. I just knew Aaron was still alive even when they told us he wouldn't live through the night. Now, they said he would never be out of a wheelchair and be handicapped. UK did a wonderful job keeping him alive, and now we're going to Cardinal Hill to give him a chance to walk, talk, and think normally again.

Once Aaron started showing signs of movement from his comatose vegetation state, the doctors and the team saw Aaron progressing faster than normal. They told us what was next for Aaron's recovery. He was going to be moved to Cardinal Hill Rehabilitation Hospital. Cardinal Hill is the best rehabilitation hospital in Kentucky and one of the best in the United States.

Doctor Silke Bernert, one of the best brain doctors (neurologists), happened to work there. We had to wait for an opening at the rehab facility and prepare for the ambulance to transport him, but now we knew our next step on Aaron's road to recovery.

When the time came to leave UK Hospital, everything seemed to move in slow motion. The UK staff loaded Aaron into the back of an ambulance for the short trip. Two medical personnel rode in the back of the ambulance with Aaron. I rode in front with the ambulance driver, and off we went to Cardinal Hill.

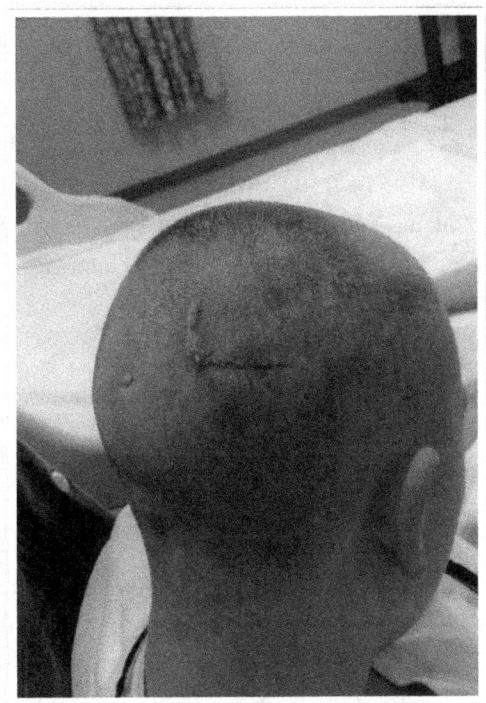

Laceration on Aaron's head from piece of metal

The ride from UK Hospital to the rehab facility was only ten minutes, but it seemed to last forever. On the ride to Cardinal Hill, I never said a word to the driver or the staff. I had a feeling inside I cannot describe. It wasn't a happy or good feeling, I just kept staring out the window, feeling sad and lonely. I don't know what it was; maybe it was because I was leaving a place I had grown to trust, and now we were going to a new place full of uncertainty, but for me, it was the longest ride. I didn't think we would ever arrive at Cardinal Hill. I guess the unknown future was why I was so sad and lonely inside.

When we finally arrived at Cardinal Hill, the ambulance staff dropped us off in an empty room behind closed doors in the brain trauma unit. I didn't like what I was feeling. I was already lonely during the ride from UK. To me, this room was eerie; it was empty, and on top of that, no one was around. We were all alone, just Aaron and me, and it felt awful. We sat in that empty room with nothing in it, and I just thought, "Well, they've left us over here to die."

It took 45 minutes, what felt like an eternity, and then the staff, the doctors, and the nurses came in to see Aaron. But when they came in, they came in like a flood! Suddenly, here they came, a large group of people: doctors, nurses, therapists. Ten or more came in there, and I was so glad to see them. The transfer from UK Hospital really made Aaron tired, and he slept for hours.

The pace at Cardinal Hill was completely different from the time we spent at UK Hospital. Everything here was happening at a much slower pace. At first, we felt like the care at Cardinal Hill was not good because the doctors and nurses were not in Aaron's room all the time, like they were at UK. But it didn't take us long to realize Cardinal Hill was the place for us to be.

Aaron was in a vegetative coma, meaning his eyes were open, and he was giving more "thumbs-up," but it was all he was doing for now. Dr. Bernert, the new neurologist, reviewed Aaron's old MRI reports and ordered new ones. There were several therapists on Aaron's team: physical, speech, and eating.

Aaron's future was so uncertain, but he was alive, and we were trying to make Aaron's life as normal as possible. At Cardinal Hill, we tried to keep to the same routine we had during Aaron's stay at UK Hospital; Veronica stayed with Aaron during the night, and I stayed during the day.

I kept the same routine as our time at UK Hospital: when I arrived at Cardinal Hill each morning, I stopped in the chapel and prayed for my family and son. I am thankful hospitals have chapels where families can go and pray in silence. Almost every night, someone would bring us dinner from a restaurant in Lexington. After Veronica came for the night, I would leave around 10:00 PM to go home and stay with our daughter Kristen.

Kristen was in college when the wreck happened and decided to take a semester off due to everything happening in our lives. After the accident, Kristen had a tough time adjusting; the whole ordeal was hard on her. She spent a lot of time alone, worrying about her brother and caring for herself. As parents, we were doing our best to keep an eye on her.

Now, she's doing well. She's married; we have a wonderful

Our daughter, Kristen Hamm, on her grandmother's front porch

Aaron and Neurologist, Silke Bernert, who we grew to love

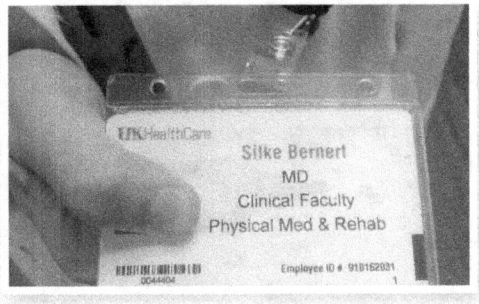

Dr. Bernert's badge

grandson and another grandchild on the way. She and her husband are hard workers.

Like her routine at UK Hospital, when Veronica arrived at Cardinal Hill to stay the night, she tuned in to K-LOVE on the radio, read scriptures over Aaron, and prayed. Veronica continued praying over Aaron for most of the night and listening to gospel music. She had very little, if any, sleep when she stayed at UK Hospital, and now it was the same at Cardinal Hill. She was faithful and committed.

One evening, Veronica arrived at Cardinal Hill around 5:00 PM. It was a little later than usual as she had a lot of business to address back home. When she arrived, Dr. Bernert spoke to us for over an hour and a half. She was wonderful.

Aaron's room consisted of a bed and a couch, and one of the nurses talked with us and told us to bring items from his room at home and make it as familiar as possible to his normal routine, which is exactly what we did. We wanted to make his hospital room look like his room at home. We brought a UK basketball, UK football items, and pictures we received from people after the accident. We also filled his room with the many thoughtful items Aaron received from friends, family, and people we knew. There were more photos of friends, get-well-soon cards, a prayer blanket gifted from a church (we used it as a cover for Aaron), and the quilt the grandmother whose granddaughter passed away had given us. We received more anointing cloths, which we pinned to his pillow like at UK Hospital.

Once again, people needed permission to come back to Aaron's room, and every day, we still had visitors, but not like we did at UK Hospital. When we were at the University of Kentucky Hospital, people would show up twenty-five to fifty at a time; at Cardinal Hill, maybe one or two families at a time. One family would leave, and ten or fifteen minutes later, another family would come and visit, but people were consistently coming to visit and pray.

More and more of his personal friends were coming over to spend time with him. The young lady he was going to pick up for the dance on the night of the wreck came to see him. More family members were spending time with him. This was our new home and our new normal for the next fifty days. I saw more people come than Veronica because I was at the hospital during the day, and fewer people visited in the evenings.

The news teams, WKYT 27 and WLEX 18, also came by Cardinal Hill for interviews. I wondered why the news stations continued covering Aaron's story. I didn't think we were special, and there were other people here with brain injuries. Nonetheless, we went and

Aaron's room for 48 days at Cardinal Hill

Aaron's special shoes; they called him Iron Man

Youth group visiting Aaron in rehab

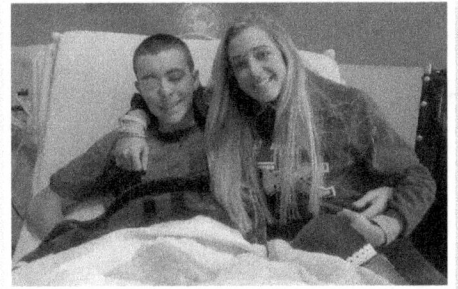
Paige Faudere visiting Aaron

did the interviews. Before ending each interview, we continued to ask Kentucky to keep praying for Aaron.

And they did! We still had visitors come to pray over Aaron. Pastors from all over the state of Kentucky, from both large and small churches, came; most were from Lexington and Mt. Sterling, Powell, and Bath

Patrick Price, news anchor, WLEX with Aaron

From Relearning Life's Basic Skills... **61**

State Representative, David Hale, with his wife, Sheila

State Pastor, Darryl Allen and his wife, Susan

Aaron and Bath County Superintendent, Harvey Tackett

Counties. I welcomed them to come and pray. It was the same as when we were at UK Hospital.

We were blessed to meet a few state officials who knew about Aaron's accident. State Representative David Hale and his wife came to visit several times. Veronica and I became close friends with our church pastor, Dr. Darryl Allen, and his wife, Susan, and we're still friends today even though they now live in Alabama.

One day, a couple of young girls, Bobbi and Mary Roe, came with their mother. They were carrying guitars and asked if they could sing a couple of songs to Aaron. Of course, I agreed. They did a beautiful job, and I still talk with them to this day. Aaron was just lying there; I don't know if he heard them, but I did.

Folks kept telling me to talk to Aaron because he could hear even though he was in a coma. He must have been able to hear because he could give a thumbs-up. When Aaron did wake up and during his recovery, I asked him if he could hear us and others speaking to him, and he said, "I didn't hear anything." I'll never really know, but I'm guessing he could.

We met so many wonderful

people who had connections to patients at Cardinal Hill. I heard all kinds of inspirational stories, and I heard many tragic stories. One thing is for sure: Veronica and I became good listeners. Person after person would tell us of their family's hardships, and we had compassion towards all those families. Something I learned was if patients weren't making any progress and it looked like they weren't going to make any progress, they sent the patient home.

The process at Cardinal Hill is if you're not improving, you're not staying at Cardinal Hill, and Aaron was improving, so they kept telling us Aaron could stay, and we could see signs of his improvement so that he could stay longer. I know a lot of people had to go home, and they weren't ready to go home, so the longer we stayed, the better we felt and believed we were going to have success.

There was one family whose teenage daughter was hurt in a sledding accident; she hit a mailbox pole headfirst. The parents would talk and pray with us, but she left Cardinal Hill in a wheelchair, unable to walk or talk. I was sad for this family whose beautiful teenage daughter was now going home in very bad condition.

I met an elderly mother whose adult daughter had fallen down a flight of stairs carrying a basket of laundry and hit her head on a wall stud; she was now at Cardinal Hill. The young lady was not improving, and they were sending her home. She was a young, unmarried businesswoman who had lived on her own. Her mother was 85 years old and lived by herself because her husband had passed away a few years ago. I remember asking her as they were preparing for her daughter to leave the hospital, "What are you going to do?"

The mother said, "I will take my daughter to my home and care for her. I don't have a choice."

I told her that would be tough. She said, "Well, what would you do?"

I replied, "I would do the same."

There was a couple in their 70s in the hospital; a lady who was with her husband, who had tried to kill himself. He shot himself in the head; he didn't die but was left badly handicapped. Now, she was taking him home to care for him. I remember her saying, "Why did he do this to me?" I was so sad for her.

One would think that at Cardinal Hill there would be less death and things would be less serious, but this was not the case. Over the intercom, "Code blue. Code blue" would ring out. I would then hear doctors and nurses running down the hall to the patient's room. I always went to the door to see what was happening. And then, I would see an EMS team take a covered body out on a stretcher with the grieving family following behind. At these moments, I knew it could be serious here at Cardinal Hill.

We heard several of these "code blue" emergencies throughout the days and nights; sadly, many didn't survive. During our stay at Cardinal Hill, we know of at least three people who died.

I often wondered if this would be Aaron's fate. Would he go home folded over in a wheelchair? Would we have to make the decision to take care of our son at home? I prayed we would not see a "code blue" response firsthand.

Aaron was still in a coma, but now his eyes were open, and even though he could not walk, talk, or move except for an occasional thumbs-up, which wasn't often or much, we were looking for more improvement. We felt blessed as Aaron slowly showed signs of continued recovery so he could stay at Cardinal Hill for more rehab.

I really don't know why, maybe because we heard about so many car wrecks, but our friend said he would like us to meet Heidi McKenzie, a young lady who had been in a wreck. I told him I would let him know, but I had forgotten about our conversation. A couple of weeks passed, and the young lady's name came up once again. He said he'd like me to speak with her. Honestly, I didn't know why. I didn't really want to talk with her; I was kind of burnt out.

He told me, "I am sure she will come and talk to you and give you some hope."

Not long after our conversation, I received a phone call; I said hello, and the caller said, "My name's Heidi McKenzie. If there is anything I could do, just let me know."

Someone else called and said, "There is a young lady paralyzed from her waist down from a car wreck. I'd like you to meet her. Her name is Heidi McKenzie."

This struck my interest. I had her number in my phone, called her back, and said, "I would like you to come to Cardinal Hill and meet Aaron, his mother, and me."

Heidi McKenzie is a remarkable young lady, and even though she is in a wheelchair, nothing stops her. She drives, snow skis, and water skis, and she has her own clothing line specifically for people confined to wheelchairs. Veronica and I fell in love with her.

During one of our conversations, she told me she has had double vision ever since her wreck, which was over eight years ago. Aaron also sees double, and I hated to think he would have double vision for the rest of his life. Cardinal Hill told us about an eye therapist, Richard Graebe, in Versailles and told us he could get rid of the double vision Aaron was experiencing. I told Heidi about him; we would see him after Aaron left Cardinal Hill. She decided to see Dr. Graebe, and she no longer sees double. She was so happy. Now, we knew there was a chance for Aaron not to have double vision. After meeting with Heidi (she was very encouraging) and showed us that disabilities don't have to stop you.

Everyone took a liking to Aaron and went the extra mile to try and help him get better. The neurologist, speech therapist, physical therapist, eating therapist, and occupational therapist all loved him. Aaron had to learn to dress, comb his hair, brush his teeth, eat, walk, and talk. The therapists were working hard with Aaron. At various times during the day, they would take Aaron to therapy, and I would go and watch to see if he was progressing.

Aaron had to learn everything all over again, just like a child. The

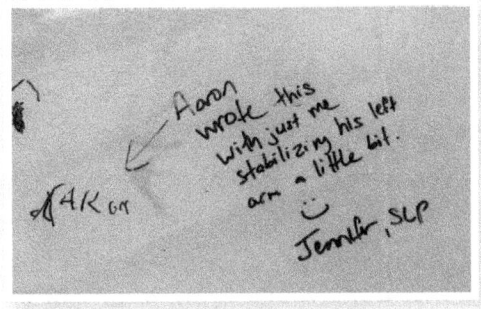

Speech therapist pointing to the first word Aaron wrote—his name

physical therapist worked on his strength. The speech therapist worked with him to talk again. The occupational therapist taught him how to do basic hygiene. These ladies looked like angels to Veronica and me. We now knew Aaron would live; however, the big question was what would his quality of life look like?

Whenever Dr. Bernert came in at Cardinal Hill, I always asked, "Is this boy going to get better?"

I asked all the therapists, "Is he going to be able to talk again? Is he going to be able to walk again? Will he be able to do things normally again?"

They'd always say, "Well, I can't answer that."

Aaron's feeding tube was removed, and he started eating and swallowing thick, cold liquids. He still couldn't walk or talk, but his feeding tube was out, and he was eating! We were thrilled the first time Aaron could stand up, and he looked so good to us, even though he couldn't stand on his own. He was strapped to a board, and then the therapist stood the board up.

The news teams were coming for interviews, visitors kept coming, and prayers continued to ring out. Aaron started eating more solid foods, he was walking with help, dressing, and brushing his teeth, and he was able to take a shower while standing with some help. He was improving; however, he was still not showing any signs of talking.

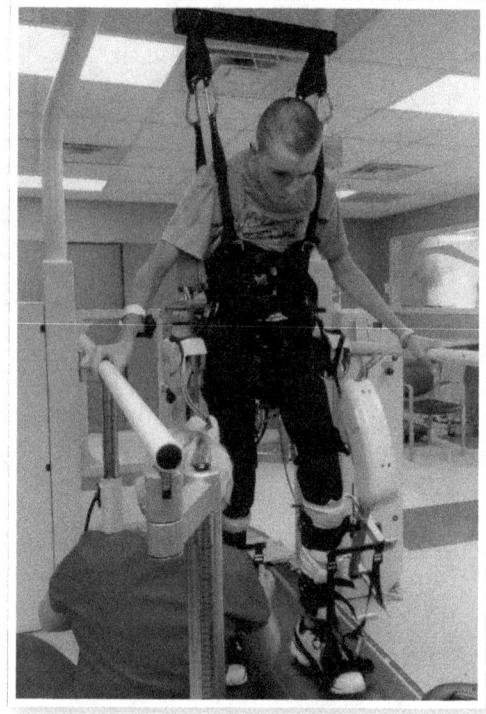

Aaron on a Lokomat Robot teaching him to walk

Even though Aaron could not talk, he still found ways to communicate with us. Aaron's favorite TV show was *The Paul Finebaum Show*, and when we tried to turn the channel Paul was on, Aaron would rattle the bed rails, which was his way of saying, "Turn it back!" These were a few funny moments during a confusing time.

As Aaron started getting better, he kept trying to tell us something but couldn't talk. We brought an iPad with us and gave it to Aaron, and he started to type and asked us all kinds of questions: What happened to me? Why am I here? Why can't I walk? Why can't I talk? The questions kept coming. Now, we could communicate with Aaron. Family and friends continued to visit, and this put a half-smile on Aaron's face; one side of his face was still paralyzed. He was finally smiling when he had visitors.

I was becoming increasingly concerned about him not talking, so I asked the speech therapist regularly, "Will he be able to talk again?"

She answered like she had before, "I can't tell you that."

Aaron was so skinny, but he was improving. At one point, I was able to start taking him down the halls, but we weren't allowed to go past the double-locked doors. Nobody with a brain injury was allowed to go past the double-locked doors; that was the door that separated brain trauma unit from the rest of the hospital. One day, they allowed us to go further than the locked doors. We couldn't stay away long, but we went through the doors to other parts of the hospital. We headed towards the elevators and went down to the basement.

The basement was quite a large area with a fountain and plants; the area was beautiful. It was a haven to relax from all the sorrow we had endured and to celebrate the victories in the hospital. I was pushing Aaron in a wheelchair, talking to him the whole time. We came across the aquarium; I stopped and showed him the goldfish and told him how beautiful it was.

Suddenly, Aaron asked, "Can we keep moving?"

"What did you just say?" I couldn't believe my ears!

"Can we keep moving?" Aaron asked.

We moved all right. I hurriedly took him back upstairs to tell his speech therapist what had just happened and thanked God for another victory in Aaron's life. Tears filled my eyes. Aaron was slowly making more progress. After so many days of heartbreak, uncertainty, and so much stress, we finally got a break from it all and saw a miracle unfold before our eyes.

As Aaron continued progressing, he had the chance to be more involved in the outside world. One day, a gentleman called us and asked if he could do a video interview with Aaron and use it at an upcoming youth convention. The expected attendance was somewhere around 800 to 1,000 kids, not counting adults. We said yes, and he and his team came to Cardinal Hill and videotaped the interview with Aaron.

Aaron was very skinny and frail, wearing a patch over one eye because of the double vision, and he still couldn't talk very well. At the end of the interview, the man told Aaron he'd like him to say two words: "Be Brave." Aaron proceeded to say, "Be strong and have courage and be brave."

The convention played the interview, and the kids yelled, "Aaron, Aaron, Aaron."

One day, a few Bath County High School administrators asked us if we

Bath County opening night of basketball season

could bring Aaron to the opening night of team practice to kick off the Bath County Wildcats basketball season. It was like Big Blue Madness at the University of Kentucky!

We had to check with his neurologist, who at first said no, it was too risky. But after time spent begging, she finally relented, "Take him straight over, then straight back. That is all!"

We agreed, and off we went to Bath County. The administration at Bath County told us what time to be there, and they were running a little late, but only by a little. The parking lot was packed with so many cars that people were parking anywhere they could. We pulled up to the gym, and a group of people were waiting for us.

Outside the gym doors, I was listening as we were helping Aaron get ready, but it was completely silent. Then, I heard the announcer say, "Junior forward Aaron Williams from Mt. Sterling, KY, playing for Bath County."

Aaron is 6 feet, 4 inches tall, long, and lean. He started playing basketball in the Upwards program and for a recreational league, in middle school, summer ball, and had private instructors. Aaron could dribble and shoot, and he was tall. Like most parents, I used to dream of Aaron going out on

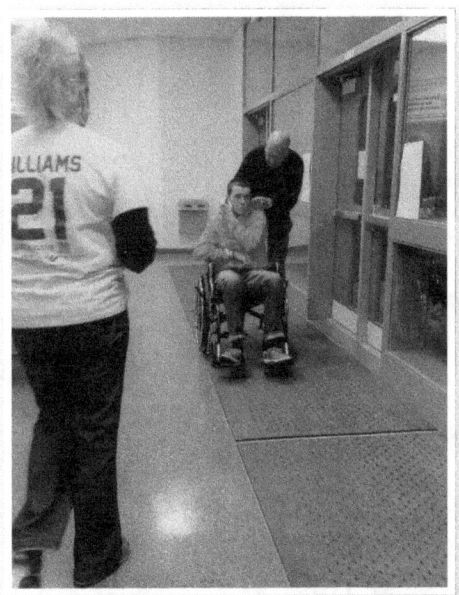
Chris with Aaron before entering basketball game

Aaron in the gym waving to everybody

the gym floor dribbling for warm-ups and the crowd cheering for my son. Well, on this night, it happened. It wasn't the way I had planned, but I could not have been any happier or prouder than when I was standing in the gym on that special night.

I pushed Aaron in his wheelchair through the gym doors held open by two of the coaching staff. Walking into the gym, I saw people everywhere, standing around the walls. Every seat was filled, and there was a roar I had never heard before. Everyone was cheering for my son, Aaron. Veronica and Kristen were with Aaron and me, and tears once again filled our eyes, but this time, it was different. Our tears of sadness once shed were now tears of happiness.

The people of Bath County are great people. After the car wreck, I regretted going to Bath County so Aaron could play ball, but not after this special night. The people of Bath County treated us like gold. Aaron worked hard to become a great basketball player, which wasn't just what I wanted. Aaron wanted it, too. He worked hard and always went the extra mile. Even after coming home from a hard practice, he would go outside and shoot the ball and run. Now Aaron was working hard again to walk, talk, and eat, to be normal again.

From Relearning Life's Basic Skills... **69**

After we had been there for an hour or so (we stayed longer than we should have, but it was such a great night for Aaron and our family), we went back to Cardinal Hill, and guess who was waiting for us: Aaron's neurologist. With a smile, she said, "Where have you all been? I hope you had a fun time."

All the nurses, from UK Hospital to Cardinal Hill, and all the doctors became attached to Aaron. I think it was because he was improving when they thought he wouldn't. Most likely, another reason they probably became attached was because Aaron was always a well-mannered, lovable boy. Over the course of time, Aaron started showing great signs of improvement. Veronica and I NOW knew he was going to be OK!

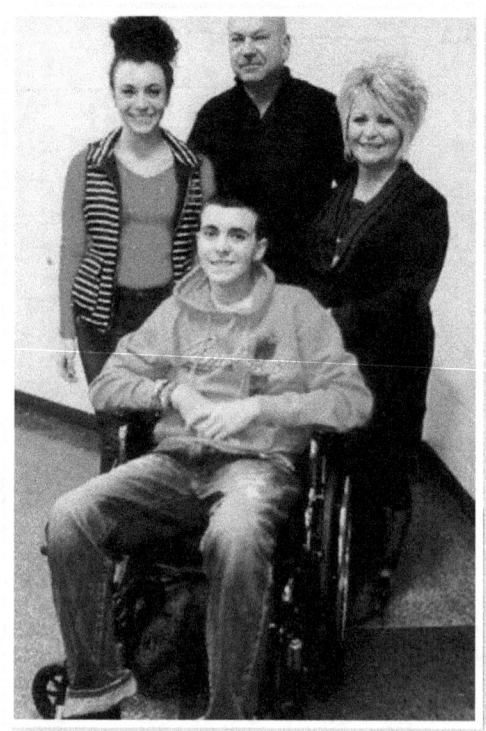

Kristen, Chris, Veronica, and Aaron after basketball event

Chapter 8
...To Aaron's Continued Recovery

"If the Spirit of Him who raised Jesus from the dead dwells in you, He who raised Christ Jesus from the dead will also give life to your mortal bodies through His Spirit who dwells in you."

ROMANS 8:11 NKJV

After 60 days at Cardinal Hill, 12 days in the ICU at UK Hospital, hundreds of visitors, and many, many more prayers, we were finally making plans for Aaron to go home. What we didn't realize was that his hospital stays were just the beginning of his future and what was to come. We didn't know what to expect when we got home. We didn't know if Aaron would be handicapped, and we didn't know how life was going to work out, but we knew he was going home.

When Aaron was still recovering at Cardinal Hill, they told us to get our home ready for Aaron's return. We hired a carpenter to make our home handicap accessible; he put handles on the door and in the showers, and we planned to make ramps for wheelchair access. But Aaron was making tremendous progress, so we had the carpenter stop the upgrades.

On the day we left Cardinal Hill, there was an emotional goodbye to all the staff and nurses. People loved Aaron, just like they always had. One of the nurses pushed Aaron down the hall in a wheelchair, and when the doors opened from the brain trauma unit, we couldn't believe what we saw. There was a line of people: doctors, nurses, and staff lining the hall all the way to the exit doors. Everyone was there, standing and applauding, all for Aaron. When we were halfway to our car, they helped Aaron out of the wheelchair and walked with him the rest of the way. If only you could have heard the cheering and thunderous applause. Veronica and I both cried.

Two sheriff cars were waiting to escort us down the bypass as we turned off the highway and onto the exit ramp for Mt. Sterling. We followed them past Montgomery County High School; they gave Aaron a hero's welcome. It was pouring down rain, but the people stood along the bypass with umbrellas in hand watching Aaron pass by. When we arrived home, our family was

Cooper Tire wearing Aaron's shirts in support

Bath County High School supporting Aaron

Whitaker Bank supporting Aaron

Back's Auto Auction supporting Aaron

Montgomery County High School supporting Aaron

waiting for us, and two news teams from the local stations were there. Aaron was home; what a miracle to have him back!

When Aaron returned home, we settled into a new routine. Veronica and I were scared because Aaron had been under the constant care of a team of doctors, nurses, therapists, and many other great hospital staff. While he was well enough to come home, he still needed care 24 hours a day. He couldn't do anything on his own. We had to watch and make sure he didn't aspirate. We had to help him take a bath, a shower, and go to the bathroom. We had to help him move everywhere he went because even though he could walk, the doctors wouldn't let him have a wheelchair because they wanted him to get back his strength. Still, it didn't matter, Aaron was home.

After a week at home, Aaron was ready to return to work gaining his strength. Just like he did when he was at Cardinal Hill, Aaron worked hard. His neurologist, Silke Bernert, developed a program at Cardinal Hill called *The Climb* Program, and she thought it would be very beneficial for Aaron.

Aaron and Veronica first day home after 60 days

The Climb Program is designed to help mentally and physically challenged patients develop and improve. Only a few patients were selected to participate. Veronica and I both wanted what was best for Aaron, so we signed him up and took the 45-minute drive to Lexington three times a week. We were used to making that drive every day while Aaron was healing in the hospital, so this was no burden for us.

During Aaron's time with *The Climb Program,* he still had issues with his double vision. Aaron

Family and friends at the house waiting for Aaron

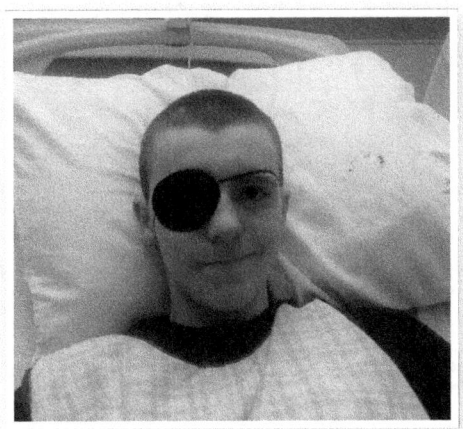

Aaron's eye patch for double vision he wore for three years

wore an eye patch to help him see better with his double vision. His favorite patch was a cheap plastic toy someone had given him. At times, when people came to visit him, they, too, would wear an eye patch. Times like these helped lift Aaron's spirits.

We had discussions and eye examinations with optometrists and ophthalmologists, all with no success. At Cardinal Hill, one of the therapists who worked in *The Climb Program* told us about an eye therapist in Versailles, KY, whom I mentioned in an earlier chapter, who works with all kinds of eye problems. We called the therapist, made an appointment, and drove to Versailles after one of his sessions at *The Climb Program* to have his eyes checked.

We faithfully took Aaron to Versailles twice a week several times and then every Wednesday for three years. It was mostly Veronica who took Aaron to the eye appointments. We told several parents whose children had eye problems, whether they were cross-eyed or had Lazy eyes; we told them about the eye doctor in Versailles, Dr. Richard Graebe, and the doctor was able to fix their eye issues. Aaron's double vision is almost gone with the special glasses his eye doctor had made for him. With the Lord's help and Dr. Graebe, only the far-left corner of Aaron's eye is affected by double vision.

Chapter 9
From Death to Life: The Aaron Williams Story

"O Lord my God, I cried out to You and You healed me."

PSALM 30:2

On the third anniversary of the wreck, Aaron reached his highest point of recovery. Throughout Aaron's healing, we had tremendous support from our family. They came and sat with him. Our families: my brother Jeff and his wife Elizabeth Williams, my mother Nancy Truskowski, and Veronica's family (Bynam, Virgie, Lanny, Betty, Pam, Shirley, Dottie, Denise, Frank, and Glenna), too many to name, were all supportive. It's good to have family support. Friends were an essential part of that encouragement and support as well. We had help through family and friends coming over, bringing us food, providing moral support, and sometimes giving us money for medical bills. Epperson Church of God, the church we attend was incredibly good to us. It's the way church should be. We hadn't known anybody who had been through a trauma like this, but we know folks who have a lot of problems. So, nobody really knew the answer to all of this, but they knew God was the answer. Now, we were faced with Aaron's continued recovery.

Aaron's neurologist said it would be good therapy for him to do extra physical exercise. Since he loved basketball, I wanted him to start going to

Mike Crow of Powell County helping Aaron with basketball skills

a gym. A good friend told us about Mike Crowe, a retired basketball coach who lives in nearby Powell County. I called Mike to ask if he would work with Aaron. He admitted he was nervous about working with Aaron but said he would. The Stanton Christian Church let us use their gym free of charge, and Mike started working with Aaron.

At the start, Aaron couldn't dribble or jump, and I mention that because when Mike first walked into the gym, he threw the ball toward Aaron, hitting him in the chest. I told Mike, "He can't do anything." Mike said he didn't realize. Aaron was a long way from touching the bottom of the backboard. He couldn't dribble; the ball rolled off his hands when he tried. He couldn't shoot or even do a layup, but Mike worked with him for two hours once a week for two years. Mike said he would look up how to work with people with brain injuries. He was good with Aaron.

While the goal wasn't for Aaron to get back into basketball, after two years of challenging work running, pushing, shooting, and dribbling, Aaron wasn't the ballplayer he once was, but now he could touch the rim, shoot three-pointers, and dribble between his legs. It was good physical and mental therapy for him to return to the gym. Mike Crowe still lives in Powell County, and he told me working with Aaron was the most rewarding work he had ever done. Even though he was initially nervous working with Aaron, Mike is so proud of him. We're so grateful to Mike Crowe.

Throughout his recovery, Aaron's story continued to be shared across the state, the country, and the world. In the hospital, when Aaron was in a coma or recovering at Cardinal Hill, most of the time, he didn't know about the reporters and news stories about him. Now that he was home, he was able to see his story shared. WLEX 18 News wanted to know when Aaron's first day going back to school was. They wanted to do a story on him and show him walking down the halls. We let them know, and they came to our house the morning he started back to school, followed Aaron to school, went inside with him, and followed him down the hallway to his first class. Several other TV shows called, and a local show came to Mt. Sterling, and the interview appeared on WLEX 18 and other TV programs.

A magazine out of South Carolina came to Mt. Sterling, wrote a wonderful story, and videotaped Aaron. The story hit the magazine stand and TV in South Carolina. We still have a drive-in theatre in Mt. Sterling, and they set aside a special night to show the story about Aaron.

WKYT and WLEX welcoming Aaron home

The 700 Club interviewing Aaron at home

The 700 Club, a national TV show, wanted to do a story on Aaron. We agreed, and they came to the house and told a remarkable story about Aaron's journey. You can still see the story by going to *The 700 Club* website. **Fighting for Life With Thousands of Prayers** (https://www1.cbn.com/fighting-life-thousands-prayers).

Just like when Aaron was in the hospital, when we asked what was going on in Mt. Sterling, people responded, "What's 'going on' is Aaron Williams." Everyone was inspired by his story; people wanted to see Aaron and hear his story. We received so many good wishes and prayers. Whenever we went out, whether to church or to dinner, it didn't matter; people asked about Aaron. I remember going to a Mexican restaurant in Mt. Sterling, and the staff wanted a picture with Aaron. So, the manager called all the employees to gather around Aaron for a picture. To this day, people often ask us about Aaron.

A group of motorcycle riders held a fundraiser ride in honor of Aaron. It was a special day. I'm not

Motorcycle fundraiser for Aaron

particularly fond of loud noises, but I had never heard a more beautiful sound when all the bikes started their engines.

We had a call from Governor Matt Bevin's office saying they would like to meet Aaron. It was very exciting, so we headed to Frankfort after some planning. It was a great and memorable day for our family.

Tom Leach is the announcer for the University of Kentucky football and basketball games. He has a program called *The All Resilient Team,* which consists of student-athletes who have overcome insurmountable odds and returned to their sport. Aaron will never be able to return to basketball, the sport he loves so

Aaron and Kentucky Governor Matt Bevin

Aaron and Tom Leach "All Resilient Team"

Crash Survivor Nominated For Tom Leach's "All Resilient Team"

Posted: Apr 12, 2016 10:52 PM EDT
Updated: Apr 12, 2016 10:52 PM EDT

The Bath County teen that nearly died after a fiery crash is one of the 25 students nominated for voice of the Wildcats, Tom Leach's "All Resilient Team" for 2016.

Aaron Williams had many broken bones, a serious brain injury and much, but he did make Tom Leach's "All Resilient Team." We headed to Louisville for Aaron to receive this great honor.

Our local Chamber of Commerce in Mt. Sterling, KY, decided to make Aaron the Grand Marshall for our annual Christmas parade. We all had a wonderful time.

Today, Aaron is a young man, but in a different way than before the accident. He's not the same, but he's normal. And he fights through it every day. When Aaron went back to school, he was as normal as he could be. After his accident, he couldn't play basketball, but he did join the Bath County Fishing Team. Aaron graduated from Bath County High School. After high school, Aaron attended the University of Kentucky, close to the UK Hospital, where he stayed in the ICU for 12 days. I consider this accomplishment a miracle. Aaron started attending Morehead State University in January 2024, changing his major to become a lawyer.

Aaron can basically do anything he wants. Aaron is our boy, and Veronica and I can tell he's a little slower than before the accident, but he can do anything he wants. If you didn't know he had a brain injury, you'd never

Aaron's graduation with his sister Kristen

Aaron playing basketball with Austin Willis

Aaron loves to fish

know. He's that good. Aaron loves fishing and hunting. He still plays some pickup basketball as he plays a lot with one of his friends, Austin.

Aaron is an incredibly positive young man. Aaron's work ethic has always exceeded other people's work ethic. Before the accident, he played ball all summer, AAU ball, and worked harder, was in the gym earlier, and stayed later than anyone. He is just that type of boy, and he worked hard with Mike after the accident even though he was limited in what he could do.

He never, ever got discouraged. He never complains; still, he doesn't complain to this day. If we said, "Aaron, we must get up at six, we have to be at therapy at eight in Versailles, he just got up and got ready."

He never, ever said, "I'm not going."

After the accident, his right side was just like somebody who had a stroke. Aaron is right-side dominant, and to this day, he doesn't quite have the full speed back on his right side, but it is very close. His left side has speed, his right side doesn't. He's about 90 percent. You can hardly read his writing, and it takes him a long time to write, and it's the one thing that hurt him in college: writing. But he knows how to type well.

He'd do anything with his right arm and leg to strengthen and improve. He'd run, workout, and play ball. It was amazing to watch him shoot his ball. He would run in our backyard and make Veronica film him so he could watch himself. He'd go again, and Veronica would film him again until he got it down.

I'd watch him fall and want to run out there and pick him up, but that wasn't the thing to do. He'd pick himself up and start running again, but it was heartbreaking when I watched him fall because he fell a lot trying to run. I was afraid he was going to hit his head. He cannot get hit in the head; it would set him back. His work ethic is still great to this day.

But he does realize he's not the same. He's never, ever said, "I can't do it because of my brain injury."

This year, he's realizing that college will be a little more challenging, but he always says he can do it.

The most notable difference is that he needs a physical and an eye exam from his medical doctors. If he passes and they approve it, the forms are sent from the Department of Transportation to Kentucky's state capitol, Frankfort, and they must sign off on it so he can still have a driver's license. At first, Aaron had to go yearly for his license renewal, but now it's every two years. Veronica and Aaron would go to Frankfort to sit in front of 20 doctors and lawyers for them to sign off so Aaron could drive.

Our journey with Aaron throughout his recovery has taught us all about ourselves. We can do all things through Christ, who strengthens us.

One side effect that affects people with brain injuries is the patients can become really angry, and Aaron got that way at times. I know some who have gotten violent; we've heard that a lot from other parents.

When he used to get angry, his eyes got big; we knew something was coming. We would try to calm him down, knowing this was just his brain injury. We didn't want him to hurt himself or others. But today, he's good. And for the most part, he's very gentle and kind. He can't handle it being too hot or cold outside.

It's not been smooth for us at times, but that is true with all families, and all parents have moments with their kids. Not long after his accident, I remember going to Dollywood with the family. It was extremely hot that day, and Aaron didn't handle it very well. It was bad. So, this has not been smooth sailing even though our life is back to normal, our new normal. To this day, we still battle issues that come up, but we deal with them, we manage them and, for the most part, everything is good. Aaron is still a great young man.

Thanks to God, I can again say if there ever was a perfect son, Aaron is it. Hopefully, we can be of help to someone who is having an extremely difficult time always have faith in God.

One day, I'm going to have to leave him because I'm getting older, and death is inevitable. I just hope I've prepared him enough that he can live the rest of his days as a responsible adult, and that's what we're trying to do: prepare him to live; he's hopefully going to get married one day; he's going to meet a special girl who will understand his brain injury. It will take a special young lady, but I know God has someone in store for him.

Aaron's story is inspirational; we started receiving invitations to special events and many requests to speak. Many local schools asked us to speak to the students, and several churches called, and we spoke at the Sunday morning worship services. We've shared Aaron's story at several places, some of which include The Upwards Program closing ceremony, the Fellowship of Christian Athletes, and church camps. Aaron and Veronica have both had speaking engagements, including several churches. We've had our share of speaking events to tell Aaron's story, and it's something I want to continue.

When I speak with a group, I take props with me. One of the props is the blanket a grandmother made for her granddaughter, which I mentioned earlier. I always take the handmade quilt because I think it's so special.

Aaron speaking at a Christian camp

After Aaron's accident, I had his car placed on a trailer in our front yard next to a "Pray for Aaron" sign. A retired state trooper lives near us, and his two boys are also state troopers, the Zalone family. I pulled that car in the front yard, and he said, "We know when we come up on a crash whether somebody lives or not. That car, there's no probable way that he lived through that. I've seen less severe crashes where people died. There's no way that boy lived through that."

That was something to hear, a big statement from a state trooper who knew what to expect when he saw a car wreck.

So, I started pulling that car to every speaking event and pulling it to Veronica's speaking events. I pulled that car everywhere with a trailer to let people know someone could survive. When people saw that car, they couldn't believe he even lived through the wreck; they said, "There's just no way. It had to be a miracle."

The ultimate goal of this book is to try and help somebody. It's the main reason I wanted to share Aaron's journey from death to life. I had been approached several times to write a book, and I always said, "No."

But we still receive calls from people with brain injuries. There was a girl on the parkway who had an accident, and she had a brain injury. When they pulled up, the first responders said she was hanging halfway out of the car through

Aaron's car burning

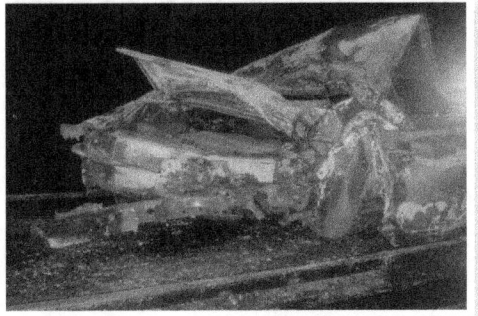

Burnt car after hitting a tree

the windshield. She has lifelong injuries, she's in a wheelchair. Her family called us to come over to meet her and share our experiences.

Finally, something just kicked in, "Why not write a book if it'll help somebody?"

So, I try to help people. That's what I do. I try to help somebody else when we go through this stuff; it's all we can do. These life lessons go further than just our experience with Aaron. I've learned to be a better parent to Kristen and Aaron. I've learned to be a better husband to my wife, Veronica. I've learned to be a better friend to my neighbor.

During the accident, Kristen went through a little rebellious spell. It was very tough and trying for us. Now, she's accepted Jesus as her savior and is a great wife and mother. Those experiences with Kristen have given me the ability to help other people with prodigal children.

I call them the prodigal child because the bible tells of a prodigal son. One thing I've learned about children is they're dependent, then they become independent, but 95 percent of the time, they come back dependent on you again. Those independent years are tough when they think they know it all and are invincible. You have to make it through the independent years. They'll come back if you can get through that part. So, for each thing that we go through, we may not like it, but we can help somebody else who has had the same problems.

I know many parents who have lost their children. I watch the news and see senseless murders of young children and teenagers. I have seen and heard of children with cancer who do not survive. Many young people have lost their lives to car wrecks. My heart aches for those parents and grandparents, but I also know of victory stories. God still heals and touches lives, and He turns sorrow into joy. He provides a light at the end of a dark tunnel. I do the best I can to stay in line with heaven. I do not only have lip service, but I also have heart service.

Some people say they hate getting old. I say, "I'm glad to experience it; the aches and pains, the tired days and getting up sore. I'm glad to experience what old age is going to be like, so I'm not complaining about old age. I can't work like I used to, I can't go as I used, but I'm glad to be experiencing it, and I'm glad to be able to experience this process with Aaron."

It would have been easier if he hadn't had the wreck, but it can't be helped.

Veronica, Kristen, and I are different. I tighten up every time an ambulance comes down the road now; every time I hear about a car wreck, I tighten up. I'm changed. I'm more nervous, and Veronica is too. I think every new sore or bump, well, cancer's back. It may not be. It's just a swollen lymph node; I hope it's only an infection somewhere. I feel good, but troubles and trials change you, and that's the thing about it. Some are for the good and some not necessarily for the good. All things work together for the good of those who love the Lord.

You never know when you will have to call on God in a terrible situation. I want people who have trouble to call me, and I will pray for them. God has decided to touch Aaron, and I believe God heard the prayers of thousands of people asking God to touch my son. I also believe God heals all believers: some on this side and some on the other side, but they are healed. For a long time, Aaron was not the boy he used to be after the car wreck. Now he's so close it is hard for his mother and me to tell. Aaron may not be fully healed here, but he will be fully healed in heaven.

Our son, Aaron, is a miracle from God. You may not believe in miracles, but I do. Aaron was not given a good outlook to live when he had the crash, but he did. Then, we were told he would be mentally and physically handicapped for the rest of his life. He's not. We have our moments, but it's worth it if we can help someone.

To this day, I think back to what the St. Joseph's Hospital nurse said when she first saw Aaron. She said you could feel the presence of God when he was brought into the emergency room. I think it has always been the providence of God to spare his life. To this day, I believe that. I also believe the man who said Aaron was chosen. We don't know what will happen tomorrow, but I'm glad I know who holds tomorrow, and I can go to God when life deals us with troublesome times.

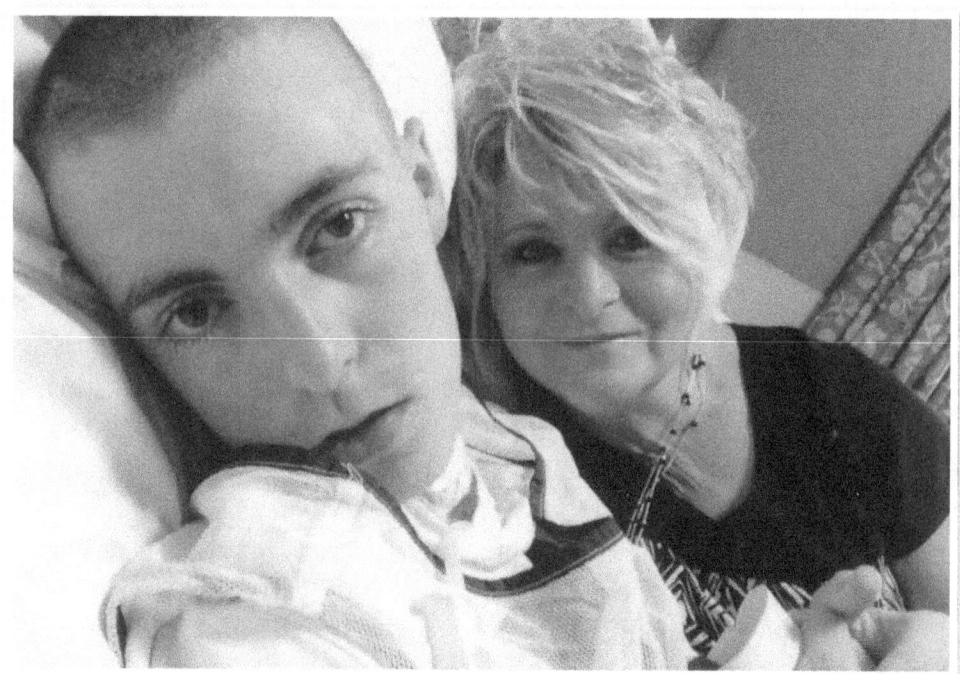

Veronica lying in bed with Aaron at Cardinal Hill

From death – picture from hospital with his mom

To Life

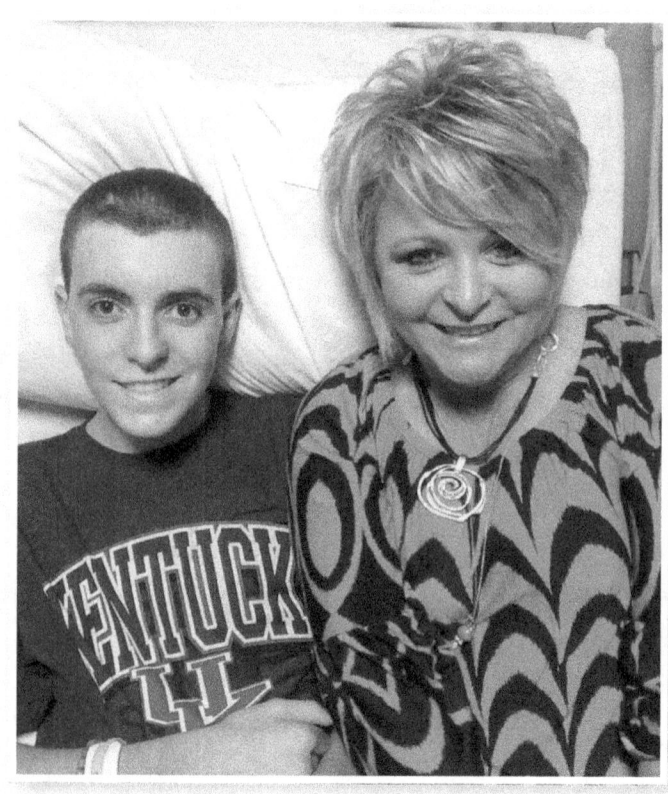

Aaron's picture Today.

Family picture

"Weeping may endure for a night, but joy comes in the morning."
PSALM 30:5

Acknowledgments

Most of all, I want to acknowledge our Lord God for giving us strength through Aaron's most challenging times and for continuing to guide us always.

My deepest gratitude to all the doctors and nurses for their care, compassion, and guidance and for not giving up when Aaron was at his worst.

To the thousands who prayed for Aaron, their vigils, visits, and never-ending faith.

To the news stations for keeping Aaron's story alive so people did not forget.

Thank you to my editors and publishing professionals, Peter and Colleen Wietmarschen, for helping me refine my manuscript for print and guiding this book through the publication process.

Thank you to Wendy Dunning for the book's cover and interior book design.

A special thank you to my wife, Veronica, for standing by me as I wrote this story and for her faith in God.

Appendix

"O Lord my God, I cried out to You and You healed me."

PSALM 30:2

Bible Verses and Other Prayers by Veronica. The Bible verses were all taken from the New King James Version online https://www.kingjamesbibleonline.org/ and NKJV physical bible.

Prayers written by Veronica
Pray to Jesus for a Healing Because He Hears You.
There are going to be times in your life when you'll need God to heal you or a loved one, so don't be afraid to PRAY to God for the healing that you need.

God heals – and He is the great physician, and He can heal anyone of any affliction, whether it be physical, mental, emotional, or financial.

Cry out to God
Cry out in the name of Jesus
There is power in the name of Jesus!
Trust in His Timing
Rely on His Promises
Wait for His Answers
Believe in His Miracles
Rejoice in His Goodness
Relax in His Presence

Diary Writings from Veronica
Journal thoughts September 19-November 5, 2015

SATURDAY, SEPTEMBER 19, 2015 – 6:15 PM
Epperson First Church of God was coming home from Cincinnati Zoo; we were in Georgetown and Claudette Faudere called at 6:38 PM and gave me the news Aaron was in an automobile accident. They (Bath County Ambulance) took him to St. Joseph Hospital in Mt. Sterling. They were going to transport him to a UK Hospital via helicopter, but the weather was not good for flying, so he was taken by ambulance to the UK.

He was taken from the emergency room to the 6th floor tower, 200 Head Trauma Unit.

He has a 3-inch cut on the back of his head to the skull, a fracture, concussion, fracture to the skull by his eye, a broken collarbone, broken rib, bruised lunch, kidney damage, and a brain injury: Diffuse Axonal Injury (DAI).

He is in a coma with no medicine. The first 24 hours were my nightmare you never want in your life. The support from all our friends and family is unbelievable.

The emergency room was full, day 1 full, day 2 full, and on day 3, we stopped visitation. There was no head count, but there were two to three hundred people, food, support, clothes, anointed clothes, blankets, money, and most of all, the world was united in PRAYER.

SUNDAY, SEPTEMBER 20, 2015 – DAY 1
Aaron was very bad today. We let visitors in way too much. But we were not sure if he was going to make it. All of his injuries were going to heal fine; just waiting on the brain to heal. Slow process.

Kim Dice gave me a necklace with a mustard seed in it to wear until Aaron got better. This is also at the beginning of Chapter 7:

"Truly I tell you, if you have faith as small as a mustard seed, you can say to this mountain, 'move from here to there,' and it will move. Nothing will be impossible for you." Matthew 17:20 New King James Version

MONDAY, SEPTEMBER 21, 2015 – DAY 2
Fever 104 degrees with double pneumonia. Aaron took a turn backward and we stopped all visitors. Bad day.

TUESDAY, SEPTEMBER 22, 2015 – DAY 3
Really having a hard day. Need Aaron right now. I went home to shower, and there was a prayer vigil at the soccer field, and several people were anointed and gathered around my house, praying to the devil away and protect us. Aaron, to me, was not there, and I felt hopeless.

WEDNESDAY, SEPTEMBER 23, 2015 – DAY 4
I am really having a bad day. Aaron is making progress, but his momma wants it now! Kristen called having a complete meltdown, saying, "Mom, when are you coming home? I need you now." I went home and my girl was at her lowest time. Pray, pray, pray, pray. We both felt better.

THURSDAY, SEPTEMBER 24, 2015 – DAY 5
Chris comes through the door in Aaron's room; very fidgety. He said something is going to happen today and I don't feel easy. I don't know if it's a good or a bad feeling. But it was a good day. His catheter came out of his head, no swelling, no fluid on the brain.

FRIDAY, SEPTEMBER 25, 2015 – DAY 6
"The thief does not come except to steal, and to kill, and to destroy. I have come that they may have life, and that they will have to have it more abundantly." John 10:10 New King James Version

Today started out well. The neurosurgeons walked into the IC Unit and passed Aaron by; the nurse said they didn't need to see Aaron anymore.

L1 and L3 lumbar fracture
Injured kidney
Top left fractured rib
Right broken collarbone
Fractured bone around the right eye
Fractured occipital bone
Cut in the back of his head

Concussion
Brain Bleed
Diffuse Axonal Injury (DAI)
Bruised lung

SATURDAY, SEPTEMBER 26, 2015 – DAY 7
Kathy Embs brought us breakfast at 8:15 AM; delicious. Aaron still has a fever of 104 degrees and pneumonia. He is off the ventilator but became very tired, so he is back on the ventilatory. Lots of visitors started coming at 8:15 AM until 8:45 PM. I finally got some sleep. I cannot even name who has been here for Aaron; too many to name. He had a special visitor, James Backer (basketball).

SUNDAY, SEPTEMBER 27, 2015 – DAY 8
I had a lot of fatigue and slept through Aaron's bath. That's OK. Aaron's fever has gone down to 98.6 degrees, and he had a small bowel movement. Now his fever is back up to 100.6. His eyes opened, and he looked at me. Chris came at 8 AM and we stayed together for one hour, and I went home to be with Kristen, Oreo, and Ellie. I had a good day with good feelings. Stopped to get gas at BP and saw a nail in the tire. Went home and got Kristen's car; she was with me. I came to the hospital, and I remember who was here—so many visitors. I am having some anxiety. I need Aaron now.

MONDAY, SEPTEMBER 28, 2015 – DAY 9
Aaron goes so deep asleep it takes 30 minutes to get a thumbs-up. I know God has been with me the whole way through this. Chris came in at 8:30 and said to go home. I stay during the daytime. I went home, and the money coming in for bills was amazing. Chris had lots of company again. Aaron had a great evening with Deadra Stone; we laughed with him at his response to us.

TUESDAY, SEPTEMBER 29, 2015 – DAY 10
Today, the physical therapist sat Aaron up in bed. Very sad to see my son this way, but God has got this, I know, but it is still heartbreaking to see. Went home to be with my baby girl Kristen. They moved Aaron to the 7th floor, Room 125, Trauma Acute ICU. A girl from Starbucks, where I would stop every morning and get coffee made Aaron a blanket.

WEDNESDAY, SEPTEMBER 30, 2015 – DAY 11
One night in the new room and the nurses let him sleep all night. Had a good day. It is very scary not knowing what is next for Aaron.
   "He heals the brokenhearted and bonds up their wounds." Psalm 147:3

THURSDAY, OCTOBER 1, 2015 – DAY 12
Aaron was moved to Cardinal Hill at 3:30 PM. Dad rode in the ambulance with him. The trip really made Aaron tired. He slept for hours while we watched him sleep. We felt like Cardinal Hill was not good because the nurses were not in his room all the time. At UK they were with Aaron around the clock (24 hours), but we realized UK was saving his life and Cardinal Hill is rehabbing him.

FRIDAY, OCTOBER 2, 2015 – DAY 13
Aaron's move made him very tired. There was not much movement from him. Scary night. Scary Day. We thought Aaron was going backward.

SATURDAY, OCTOBER 3, 2015 – DAY 14
Spent the day with Kristen.

SUNDAY, OCTOBER 4, 2015 – DAY 15
Jake Purus wanted to do a motorcycle run for Aaron behind the Downtown Athletic Club. Registration started at 2:00; left for the ride started at 3:30.

MONDAY, OCTOBER 5, 2015 – DAY 16
My first day back to work after 16 days; hard day.

TUESDAY, OCTOBER 6, 2015 – DAY 17
Aaron had his first day all by himself and he had great therapy.

WEDNESDAY, OCTOBER 7, 2015 – DAY 18
I stayed for Aaron's therapy, and it was great!

THURSDAY, OCTOBER 8, 2015 – DAY 19

Aaron was alone in therapy again. Julie Clark and her mother came by, and he was out in the hall at the nurse's desk in the blue chair. Aaron had lots of company again and WKYT 27 came and did an interview with Chris.

"Behold, I give unto you power to tread on serpents and scorpions, and over all the power of the enemy: and nothing shall by any means hurt you." Luke 10:19 - New King James Version

FRIDAY, OCTOBER 9, 2015 – DAY 20

Left at 6:00 AM to go to work. Went to work and stayed with Kristen. We came back to the hospital at 6 PM. Aaron was tired from all of his company. He slept all night. Still not walking or talking. I got to give Aaron ice chips for the first time, and he ate one-half cup of ice, and he swallowed it all. Thank you, Lord!

SATURDAY, OCTOBER 10, 2015 – DAY 21

Left Aaron at 8 AM. Aaron was asleep. I did not want to leave, but I had to work and go see Mom, Dad, Denise, and Darvin. Darvin was very sick from treatment. Had a day with only crying one time. Brought Mom, Pam, Kristen, and Ryan back to the hospital with me. Aaron had just come back from his shower and was very tired.

Love the song today, "Loyal" by Lauren Daigle.

SUNDAY, OCTOBER 11, 2015 – DAY 22

I stayed with Aaron all day except when Chris and Kristen came over, and Kristen and I went to the mall for her to show with her mommy. Had a good day. Aaron had over 15 visitors today; lots of company.

TUESDAY, OCTOBER 13, 2015 – DAY 24

I left for work at 6 AM and Chris came at 6:30 AM. Aaron had another good day. I came back at 4:30 PM and brought Kristen and Ryan with me. Aaron also had his trachea removed. He passed his swallowing test.

WEDNESDAY, OCTOBER 14, 2015 – DAY 25

I stayed the night and all day. Aaron had his first meal – sausage gravy, eggs and peppers, oatmeal, banana, milk, and apple juice. He ate 80 percent of his food. Lunch was just a few bites because breakfast wore him out. He ate 70 percent of dinner.

THURSDAY, OCTOBER 15, 2015 – DAY 26

Left for work at 6 AM. Today, Aaron was put on a robot that walked and monitored him. He took 25 steps of his own.

FRIDAY, OCTOBER 16, 2015 – DAY 27

Left for work at 6 AM and Chris came at 7:30 AM. Aaron had occupational therapy (OT), physical therapy, and ST, but he seems very tired. Sleeps a lot.

SATURDAY, OCTOBER 17, 2015 – DAY 28

I left Aaron at 6 AM to go to work, Chris went deer hunting in Frankfort. He said he couldn't hunt because he was thinking of Aaron. Everyone at work is so wonderful to me. They bring me food and money all the time. Tried to meet Larry Carper again. No luck. Went home and spent some time with Kristen and we had a very good day. Kristen needed me to order Ryan a one-year gift (wallet and coin holder).

I came back to Aaron about 6 PM and we had a good night. We took some selfies of ourselves, and I was lying in his bed, but he let me for just a little while then pushed me out.

He slept most of the night. His condom catheter came off, so he wet everything and had to be changed at 2:30 AM. Today I would love to see Aaron try to speak. In Jesus' name, Amen.

SUNDAY, OCTOBER 18, 2015 – DAY 29

Doctors came in to check Aaron at 6:15 AM. Aaron had a busy day. At 11 AM Stephanie, Brad, Taylor, Peyton, and a friend McCarty came. Then Paige and Claudette Faudere, Tony, Tracy, Natalie Pesina, Albert, Tammy, Megan, Jace Burton and Ann and Isaac Hollon.

MONDAY, OCTOBER 19, 2015 – DAY 30
Left for work at 6 AM. Worked til 3:30 PM and spent time with Kristen, and she went to school, and I came back to Cardinal Hill. Aaron had a good day. He tried to sit up by himself.

TUESDAY, OCTOBER 20, 2015 – DAY 31
Stayed all day with Aaron. He was put on a robot to walk on a treadmill. He did 30 percent of the motion. He ate 100 percent of his food. Dr. Bernert came in Aaron's room and recommended he go on a stimulant medicine (Ritalin) to wake him up more to speed up his recovery. The risks are high blood pressure and seizures which can be fatal. He began his new medicine at 2:30. He was very restless. The Occupational Therapist, Cassie, had Aaron play air hockey and that was great!

WEDNESDAY, OCTOBER 21, 2015 – DAY 32
Left Aaron at 6 AM to go to work on my new schedule. Aaron, with the help of two people walked 200 feet with one break. He ate in the cafeteria with his speech therapist (Jennifer). She fed him his meal.

THURSDAY, OCTOBER 22, 2015 – DAY 33
Aaron had physical therapy at 9 AM on the Lokomat (robotic rehabilitation device) donated by Dusty Hicks' parents.

FRIDAY, OCTOBER 23, 2015 – DAY 34
Went to work, left Aaron at 6 AM, he was asleep. Came back at 6 PM. Ryan and Kristen came with me while Chris worked at Back's Auction. Kathy Embs came over and took Kristen and Ryan home for me.

SATURDAY, OCTOBER 24, 2015 – DAY 35
Left Aaron at 6 AM to go to work. Came back at 4 PM with Kristen and Ryan and we went to the mall for Kristen's birthday shopping.

SUNDAY, OCTOBER 25, 2015 – DAY 36
Left Aaron at 8:45 AM after I fed him breakfast to go to First Baptist to speak about what GOD has done for Aaron Williams and then came back to the hospital. Aaron had a very active day. A lady named Patti Wooner brought home dinner for us. She heard our story on TV.

MONDAY, OCTOBER 26, 2015 – DAY 37
I went to work, and Chris stayed with Aaron today. Chris is very agitated today and wants things back to normal.

TUESDAY, OCTOBER 27, 2015 – DAY 38
Had to go home at 9:00. Chris was angry again.

WEDNESDAY, OCTOBER 28, 2015 – DAY 39
Worked.

THURSDAY, OCTOBER 29, 2015 – DAY 40
Aaron told the speech he was not going to make it. The nurse had to tell Aaron to calm down.

FRIDAY, OCTOBER 30, 2015 – DAY 41
Kim Dice came to the shop and asked me, "What can I get you?" I responded by saying an iPad. This iPad was the best money I had ever spent. Aaron started talking through the typing. He had lots of questions about how he was.

SATURDAY, OCTOBER 31, 2015 – DAY 42
Aaron started talking at a whisper. This day has been the best day!

SUNDAY, NOVEMBER 1, 2015 – DAY 43
Very busy day with visitors who started coming at 10:30 AM and ended at 7:30 PM.

MONDAY, NOVEMBER 2, 2015 – DAY 44
Left for work at 6 AM. Chris came at 7 AM. Aaron had a good day.

TUESDAY, NOVEMBER 3, 2015 – DAY 45
Kristen's 19th birthday. We had a lot of people in Aaron's room to celebrate Kristen's birthday.

WEDNESDAY, NOVEMBER 4, 2015 – DAY 46
Aaron's feeding tube was removed while Chris and I were at work (:. Came back at 5:30 PM and Trevor Martin was with Aaron.

THURSDAY, NOVEMBER 5, 2015 – DAY 47
Aaron pooped and peed in the toilet, brushed his own teeth, washed his own hands, helped me change his clothes, then became lazy and said, "Feed me," so I did. Therapy is at 11. Aaron walked with the tall walker with PT; Laura helping.

About the Author

Chris Williams and his wife Veronica enjoy life with their three children, Aaron, Kristen, and Hailey, their grandchildren, and other family members. Chris is a man of faith and believes God does perform miracles. He is incredibly involved in his community in Mt. Sterling, KY. He has had several speaking engagements and interviews with different outlets, including *The 700 Club*, *Fighting for Life With Thousands of Prayers* (https://www1.cbn.com/fighting-life-thousands-prayers), Governor Matt Bevin, Tom Leach, UK football and basketball announcer, State Representative David Hale, and preachers from churches and local stations in Kentucky. Chris continues to share his story, using his voice to support families and victims of trauma. He hopes he can help someone having a challenging time always have faith in God.

www.ingramcontent.com/pod-product-compliance
Lightning Source LLC
Chambersburg PA
CBHW070343010526
44119CB00029B/413/J